MISTAKES WERE MADE

Reflections on Being a Mediocre Father

SHANE BORROWMAN

Lucky Bat Books

for John and Samantha
    who will read this eventually
        Faith

for Elizabeth
    who lived it all, plus the things that aren't
    mentioned
        Hope

for Mom and Dad
    who taught me the good things
        Love

Contents

A Note from the Author
May 2014

I still feel—kind of temporary about myself.
　　—Willy Loman in Arthur Miller's *Death of a Salesman* (Act I)

THE ESSAYS IN this collection were written between 2005 and 2014... from the time my twins, John and Samantha, were born until they were nine, the last of the single-digit years. They were originally published in a range of print and online venues (see "The Backlist" for a complete listing) and are collected here for the first time. Previously published works are modified only minimally—just in those instances where an editing error was introduced at publication, when some element of the original formatting was lost, etc.

My twins were born in Spokane, Washington, where Elizabeth and I lived while I taught at Gonzaga University, and where, depending on the year, I either ran the writing program, or ran the writing program and the tutoring center, or ran myself ragged being "just" an assistant professor. Sam and John were raised in Nevada, while I taught at the University of Nevada, Reno, and they began kindergarten at the elementary school only a handful of blocks from our home. Now, while I serve as Department of English Chair at the University of Montana Western, they have, impossibly enough, reached the end of 3rd grade.

They fish and ski, play football and soccer, ride bikes and scooters, and are a joy. More and more often, my role simply seems to be standing out of the way...ready to help two kids already mature enough and driven enough not to need everything I'd still like to give.

So I write about them…more often than they yet realize. And I obsess over my mistakes.

The list of mistakes—real or otherwise—is a long one, something unavoidable when new events are added continuously and nothing is ever removed. Ever.

Today: John receives a call from a friend, asking if he can spend the night. My wife looks at me. I look back. Shrug. "Fine with me." Samantha turns her back, begins to walk away. I can see that her elbow is bent, and I know that she's sucking her thumb, something she only does when confronted by serious anxiety. I could go to her, could comfort her, could distract her. I don't. I hate that she sucks her thumb, even though it's not unusual, even though I understand its cause.

In fact, I'm part of the cause. Describing that mistaken moment when comfort was likely needed but was not given, I remember that we talked about this several hours before. "Sam's got an appointment with the dentist on Friday," Elizabeth told me as I worked to shove one more dirty bowl into a dishwasher already over capacity (and not terribly effective even when I load it correctly). "I'll have him refit the appliance or take it out."

"Take it out," I said without even looking up from my jigsaw work, fitting a bowl with the dried remains of chocolate ice cream between a copper-bottomed sauce pan that warmed up soup and a plate stained by chicken nuggets and ketchup. "It hasn't done a thing since the day he installed it."

"The appliance" is a sort of wire mesh that fits across Sam's palate. It's designed to make sucking a thumb impossible. It fails. It's failed from the very beginning.

But I didn't have to be so blunt, not with Sam standing nearby.

Now she's upstairs, playing with a friend who is spending the night. I'll go fix their dinner soon; they've elected to have macaroni and cheese, and, nutrition be damned, I'm allowing it. I'll cut green apple and jicama to go with the carb dump. John's at a friend's home, somewhere he's stayed once or twice before. I don't think I even know the name of the parents monitoring that mini-sleepover. I know my wife knows...but that seems pretty weak.

I'll give all of these mistakes or possible mistakes or perceived mistakes more thought than they deserve. I'll ruminate on them. I'll add them to the roll, which contains everything from my poor decision to take out student loans to my current choice to eat too many potato chips...a mistake that has me up 20 lbs. and out of all but two pairs of jeans.

Two nights ago, though, I was flat on my back in the guest bed at my parents' home. It was hot, and I was on top of the covers, knowing I should take another pain pill because of the herniated disc in my back but unwilling to do so. I have no problem with better living through chemistry, but I've gone from being a very heavy drinker in my youth to a fairly light drinker (by comparison) in middle age. Taking any opiate day after day after day doesn't appeal to me long term.

I was watching *Rome*, a mediocre mini-series produced by HBO years ago to dramatize ancient Roman politics in the last days of the Republic. I'd waited through uninteresting family drama among patricians and a questionable portrayal of Cicero as a fairly odd mix of schemer and coward. The waiting paid off: Two main characters were in the arena, and weapons were a'swinging.

Then my son appeared out of nowhere, upset by a nightmare and by the fact that he couldn't find Sara Bear, the Harley Davidson clad green triceratops with an odd last name. I don't remember what he said, maybe didn't even hear him. I snapped my iPad closed, slid it down between the bed and the wall, and pulled him up against me: "Get some sleep, buddy."

John rolled until his back was against me—his sweaty skin pressed against mine, since we both sleep in sweatpants or pajama bottoms, year round—grabbed my left hand in both of his, and went to sleep almost instantly. I was trapped on my back, too hot to sleep and unable to reach my iPad...or to watch Rome, anyway, since I didn't have headphones.

I lay there, in the dark, awake much of the night. I'm not a back sleeper. John wakes up if someone moves near him or adjusts him, so I was frozen. I could smell his hair, smell the grass he'd played in all afternoon in the backyard, leaping from one inflated pool to another and back. His breathing slowed, steadied, kept me centered. No mistakes.

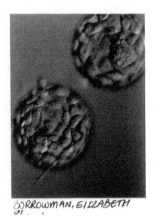

BORROWMAN, ELIZABETH

I'M AN ENGLISH professor by training and trade, but I'm not much of a grammarian. No one ever learned to be a better writer by studying decontextualized grammar, and my eyes glaze over as quickly as anyone else when arcane points of correctness are debated.

My son likes to correct people's speech, particularly when they say something like "Me and Bill went to the park."

"Bill and I," he'll immediately whisper. Everyone just assumes that he gets this moderately annoying habit from me, assumes that John's correcting grammar because I do it. But I don't. Occasionally, he'll hear me say something wildly ungrammatical and chastise me: "Dad, you're an English professor!"

"Yeah," I always respond, "but I'm not a very good one."

That seems to satisfy him. My daughter occasionally defends me: "You're ok at it, Dad."

Ask any grammarian, though, and the answer will be the same: "Mistakes Were Made" is a passive construction. It focuses on the fact that there were mistakes…not on who made them. It's an avoidance tactic, a way to acknowledge some reality without overtly taking ownership for it. It's not dishonest, exactly, just…cowardly. That's the word that comes to mind. More accurately, and actively, the sentence should read, "I made mistakes." I describe a range of them in the pages that follow, and sometimes the mistakes are corrected.

But that's another passive construction: "Sometimes mistakes are corrected."

An active description would read, "I made mistakes. I sometimes fixed them." And that's true, generally, and not just as a parent.

I never learned to balance my checkbook. I still haven't, although I at least understand, conceptually, why it's a good idea.

I remained the same weight for decades and never gave my diet a thought, regardless of the fact that beer was its most solid staple. In middle age, I have no sense of how to balance my weight—no more than I do my checkbook. As I creep toward 170 lbs., this seems like an issue. My doctor looks alarmed, which makes me at least try to pretend to vaguely care on at least part of one level. That is literally all the care I can bring to the matter, despite a total awareness of the fact that my kids are young, and both they and my wife need me in the present rather than past tense.

There are other mistakes. Some worse, in their own ways.

I spent more than a quarter of a million dollars online, buying a house based solely on a few pictures and the recommendation of my real estate agent.

I never deliberately touched a football, put on a baseball mitt, held a Frisbee, or dribbled a basketball until parenthood forced me to. Some of that probably came about because my sister was a really fine athlete. Plus, a PE teacher I might have learned a lot of this from was a perverted freak, so I spent a couple years working in a library rather than sweating in a gym. He's retired now from teaching, but several generations of kids, now grown, will probably be even happier when he's finally dead. Thankfully, he's also an alcoholic, so it shouldn't be long now.

Holding that sort of grudge nearly three decades after I last saw the guy is probably a mistake, too, but hate is something I'm pretty good at, especially pointless, mindless hate.

I once tolerated a level of workplace bullying that would never be allowed to continue in my twins' elementary school. But workplace bullying, especially in a restricted and hyper-polite environment like a university, is hard to prove. Easy to feel, though.

I was published for the first time when I was 19 or 20, which wasn't a mistake, but I probably never should have written a poem about how much I looked up to then-Secretary of Defense Dick Cheney. There's just no excuse for that, and some things are beyond apology.

Mistakes were made, persistently and chronically. But most of my mistakes are neither passive nor past tense.

I ignore the warnings on medicine bottles, blithely operating machinery and consuming alcohol with no thought to the consequences and/or side effects.

I disregard drug interactions, at least until my doctor tells me that's why I'm nearly passing out every time I stand up. Something about blood pressure medicine and a painkiller I take when "cluster headaches" show up. Apparently, a cluster headache is just like a migraine, except it can come and go with no warning. Mine went away for twenty years. I'm unclear on how this is different from a migraine.

I forget the names of my children's teachers almost the instant I learn them. I don't even recognize their teachers when they "Hi" me at Safeway.

I forget the names of my kids' friends. All of them. I don't know where most of them live, and I don't know most of the parents. My wife knows all this. I guess.

I don't always balance work and family. I fail this professional high-wire act even though a friend once noted, "Your children will never say, 'I'm glad my dad got tenure,' but they will say, 'I'm glad my dad was there.'"

I don't arrange enough date nights, despite the fact that my friend Amanda is almost always available as a babysitter.

I worry about money. Constantly. Even when I have no reason to worry...which does occasionally happen.

I foolishly had no camera at hand when Kurt Vonnegut flipped me off. Not me personally, exactly, but I was standing at the front of a group he flipped off. So he was telling everyone, collectively, what he thought, but he was looking at me, specifically. And I didn't have a camera. This wasn't all that long before his death, so I guess I'm probably not going to get another opportunity.

I lose my cellphone. A lot. And I never think to call it and chase down the ring until it's been a long, long time...and the battery's gone dead. Two conjoined mistakes.

I get cranky on any trip longer than an hour, which, in Montana, means just about every trip. I am unpleasant to be around when I'm cranky. But I refuse to let anyone else drive, since I'm a control freak. So this leaves me a cranky, exhausted driver, one almost incapable of being nice to anyone until the vehicle reaches its destination. If by some miracle I don't sit behind the wheel, I'm the worst sort of co-pilot, the kind who tries not to say anything but grabs for the door handle all the time for no rational reason.

Taking me on a trip is a mistake. It really is.

I punish myself by trying to live the diet my doctor prescribes—no sugar, no starch. Everything I like has sugar and/or starch, so I just drink a lot of tea and otherwise starve myself. Then I binge on a bacon burger, fries, and a chocolate sundae. I'm pretty sure that's not what my doctor has in mind.

I go to the trouble of planting a garden every spring and then don't regularly water it. So results are mixed at best. Whatever survives my lackluster attempts at irrigation is haphazardly harvested, so most of it goes to seed and goes to waste. Apparently, at least in my little part of Montana, lettuce thrives in a climate of drought and indifference.

While revising this introduction—literally, at the moment I was writing a more developed version than the sketchy original—my daughter asked if she could go to the skate park with two friends (my son is at camp). She doesn't know how to get to the park, but they do. I looked at my wife. No help there. I made an executive decision (never a good plan): She went to the skate park. I told her to be back in about a half hour. She wasn't home almost two hours later, but kids have a terrible sense of time, and she owns no watch. I stood on my deck and listened. No kid sounds. I started on a slow walk to find her/them, and as I turned toward the grocery store, I heard them coming up the street behind me—just a gaggle of sugar-sticky faces and laughter. I called my wife (unbelievably, I had my cell phone on me) to let her know the kid was on her way, along with her entourage, and I kept walking. I constructed a transparent lie about how I needed to walk to Safeway for a few things (chocolate and sweet tea, neither approved for my diet). It's good that she's back, but now she'll expect to be able to go off with only rubberstamp approval of a request. Oops. And John will expect to have this same privilege that Sam now enjoys once he comes home.

I should have thought that through. I did end up writing about it, however, in "The New Normal."

I tend to act without thinking quite that far ahead, though; I still manage to act surprised when the consequences appear.

I asked my son if he's ready for the 4th Grade Day One Initiation. He said he didn't know. "No worries," I told him, "as long as you've got good running shoes and a change of underwear."

Pause for effect.

"And the bear they use isn't really that big."

"You," John noted, "are a strange man."

A Note About Structure

For infinitely various are the incidents in one man's life which cannot be reduced to unity.

—Aristotle, *Poetics* VIII

MISTAKES WERE MADE is divided into two separate and unequal sections. Section one is organized in a roughly chronological order. Roughly. Because each essay was originally constructed as a stand-alone piece, however, the age of my twins jumps around a bit; something published in 2008 may have been drafted days or years before. So my own experiences of fatherhood, like the ages of my twins, move ahead in these pages by fits and starts. Section one covers the events that run from my twins' infancy through the early years of elementary school. These are, to deploy a photographic sort of metaphor, the "Images in the Foreground."

The second section of *Mistakes Were Made* is titled "Background Noise." The pieces there come from the freakishly large number of folders named "miscellaneous" or "misc" that I have on my laptop. Some of them are complete essays, polished but unpublished. Until now. In other cases, I have included journal entries and fragments of essays, things that illustrate in greater detail and depth my experiences as a husband and father. Where it's appropriate, I've provided links between the essays in section one and some relevant companion pieces in section two.

Before all of these essays, though, in section one and section two, I've included a brief bit of framing…just enough to tee up the essay to come. Or to take the opportunity to make an inappropriate joke that just didn't fit anyplace else. As a longtime writer and editor, I've obsessed over every element of this book, from "to" vs. "too" errors to vague pronoun references. Every time I look at the manuscript, however, I find more errors, and the writer in me wants to add just a little more. Just a little more here and there. This is, I've learned from experience, a bad thing.

Still, mistakes were made.

There is one mistake I've avoided as much as possible, however: While my wife Elizabeth appears in these pages, I've kept her presence to a narrative minimum. This is no reflection of reality, of my life in which she is the center, the subject, the substance. It isn't her fault she married a writer, and I won't deliberately drag her into even a dim spotlight if I can help it.

Section One:
Images in the Foreground

No one can tell what goes on in between the person you were and the person you become.

—Stephen King, *The Stand*

Only after disaster can we be resurrected.

—Chuck Palahniuk, *Fight Club*

We can't blame ourselves. It's just a bunch of little choices that don't mean anything till the shit hits the fan, and then you look back and see how you got there.

—Richard Laymon, *Dark Mountain*

"Shoot the Drift" was first drafted as I sat in a classroom at the University of Nevada, Reno. The room was filled by MA and PhD students, all enrolled in a workshop being directed by UNR's director of composition. Because I'd been hired to replace her as composition director, once I was tenured, I was sitting in, taking part in the get-to-know-you portion of the day's work. I don't remember the prompt that set things in motion, but "Shoot the Drift" was the product.

Shoot the Drift
2005

I'M ON MY knees in the dim basement, gripping a pistol in my right hand, index finger on the trigger guard. There are six shells in the clip, loaded by beer-clumsy fingers. I'm about to fire them into the man-shaped target 45 feet away. My elbows rest on the battered brown surface of a bar stool, a long-ago tear covered with electrician's tape. I blink to clear my blurry eyes and bleary mind.

"Shoot the drift" Dave says from behind my right shoulder, telling me to compensate for the pendulum swaying of my arms and shoulders, the rhythm of my breathing, the beat of my heart. I've fired rifles many times, but the drift is different with a pistol. More pronounced. Compensating for this unavoidable motion involves timing and balance—timing the shot for the moment the gun sights cross the targeted point, balancing between wanting to pull the trigger and willing my body to be patient. Dave stands behind me and instructs, knowing that the physical reality of drifting can be overcome: "Shoot the drift."

There's more here than instruction in marksmanship. Dave hunts for pleasure and reads Greek philosophy, especially Aristotle's arguments about the Golden Mean. He taught me to write and to teach others. Tonight he's teaching me to shoot a pistol, and I'm not surprised that his counsel on accuracy is applicable beyond his basement. Dave's lesson is a startlingly accurate description of the previous year.

I begin to fire. The explosive smell is sharp, chemical and machine working in harmony. Dave cares for his guns and loads his own shells. I expect, and get, perfect operation. My shots come in an irregular rhythm but all fly true. This is a great surprise to me. I'd worried about shooting badly, about disappointing Dave, about putting a shot through his wood-paneled wall and into the gas line.

Finished, I snap the safety, lay the pistol on the torn seat, check the target. We discuss the merits of various hits by pointing and shrugging with our hands. The best one goes through silhouette-man's throat, sprawling him on the floor of my imagination, a pool of blood spreading. A straight shot, despite the drift.

Before I ever put hand to pistol, there was drift in my life. Learning to compensate for it is taking everything this drunken exercise in philosophy and precision can offer.

I've drifted since Elizabeth and I began discussing adoption nearly a year before, reading manuals and how-to Web sites, wandering through the offices of lawyers and social workers, weighing open adoption versus closed versus foster care. I've drifted through the physical, financial, and emotional costs of in vitro fertilization—and through months of delivering Elizabeth's daily injections into her hips, shooting the needle in, pulling back to look for blood, plunging the oil-based hormone injection into her small body. She tells me the shots don't hurt, despite the ever-growing circles of bruises, blue-black at their centers and malarial yellow at the distant borders. I've drifted through January night false-alarm runs to the hospital and weeks of daily visits with other parents in the aggressively cheerful waiting rooms of the neo-natal intensive care unit, where most of the toys are wooden and missing parts and the liquid soap smells like pink bubblegum.

By this night on Dave's indoor and illegal shooting range, when a lesson in the physical demands of accurate marksmanship provides me with a metaphor for my confusion as a new father, the twins born of my drifting are less than four months old. I've learned to mix formula according to a doctor's instructions, enriching the mix to overcome the deprivation of premature birth. I've learned to clean the parts of a breast pump, to assemble without directions hand-me-down cribs and mobiles and car seats, to fix loose wires in a second-hand baby monitor. My office is a nursery, the desk where I write dwarfed by a crib big enough for two infants. My wife is learning to be a mother. A good mother. Our parents already know how to be grandparents, and my closest friends—including Dave—are falling naturally into their roles as aunts and uncles. I am still drifting, swaying between the man I was before and the man I am now, still hitting neither the physical nor metaphorical targets with accuracy.

But I'm learning to shoot these drifts.

"Shoot the Drift is the only essay I've ever published based on half of its value. It's been years, and I don't have the emails anymore, but the editor at Brevity said something along the lines of "We really like the first half of this and want to publish it, but the second half doesn't work." Maybe he even said it was "terrible" (and I'm just softening things in retrospect). I include that original draft because it reveals a lot more about my state of mind than does this finished product: "Shoot the Drift: Original Draft."

I grew up in the non-cable world where we received only two channels, both major network affiliates broadcast out of Butte, Montana. I watched "The Price is Right" in the morning, along with "Wheel of Fortune"—which was powerfully awesome then, primarily because winning contestants were forced to spend all of their money right then, on the spot, on objects set upon a revolving stage—merchandise that included things like electric blankets and ceramic dogs. I watched "Days of Our Lives" and sometimes "General Hospital." Everyone did. But talk shows just weren't around, not until Phil Donahue pioneered the genre, further refined by such luminaries as Ricki Lake and Morton Downey, Jr. She should have retired at the top of her game, just after filming Where the Day Takes You. *So talk shows weren't around when I was young, but I drank a lot of afternoon beers and did a catchup seminar taught by Geraldo Rivera in the early 1990s. Then I got busy for more than a decade—going to college, listening to Bruce Springsteen, whatnot. When my twins were very young, though, I suddenly found myself with a lot of time on my hands...and access to cable television.*

Sleep Deprivation, Drunkenness, and Dr. Phil
January 2013

He has that air of one who has and will spend too much of the evening teetering on the edge of consciousness but never quite passing out.
—John O'Brien, *Leaving Las Vegas*

I KNEW I was in trouble when I began planning my day around Dr. Phil. His program came on at 3:00, and I looked forward to this all day. It was the closest thing I got to adult conversation between 8:00 am and 5:00 pm.

I was thirty-five years old when John and Samantha were born. I grew up with no siblings, no young cousins, no neighbors in need of babysitting. Until March of 2005, I never changed a diaper, never mixed a bottle, never considered the implications of fatherhood. If my problem had been simple ignorance, then it wouldn't have really been a problem at all.

But my issues were bigger.

John and Samantha were premature, although, thankfully, the only disability they had to overcome was an inability to suck-swallow-breathe. This sounded simple when the doctor explained it, as I stood sweating in my hospital scrubs and nodded wisely, but in effect it meant that the kids couldn't eat without intervention—without a tube down their noses and into their stomachs. Learning to take nourishment took them four weeks.

During those weeks, the nurses in the NICU taught me the basics, the daily maintenance skills that made up, as much as possible, for a lifetime of ignorance. Then the kids came home, and my wife went back to work, and I was parenting solo for nine hours per day. Under normal circumstances, this wouldn't have mattered, but fatherhood isn't normal, as Dr. Phil quickly taught me.

As much as possible, I managed the kids at night so that my wife could rest. I wasn't working. She was. I put the crib in my home office. For the first week, I sat in my chair and surfed the web, played video games with the sound turned down, wrote. I was productive.

Every two or three hours, someone needed to be fed. Because they were premature, we were advised to mix the formula in a richer form—to help with weight gain. This was great when I got the combination of formula and milk and water just right, but that balancing act almost never happened.

Which meant that both kids would, at some point during or after each feeding, throw up. On me. On the floor. On each other. I cleaned the carpet, but the ghosts of stains past formed layer after layer of nastiness that I simply began to throw a towel over.

After that first week of taking care of two infants all night and during most of the day, I entered a state that resembled intoxication. I could think clearly, but it took longer. I could handle any physical task, but I fumbled. I stopped surfing the web and playing games. Instead, I slid my chair into the corner, lay on the floor, and watched DVDs on the computer. When watching *Rocky* became too complicated, I began to listen to Sid Vicious, Me First and the Gimme Gimmes, and Billy Joel. Quietly.

And like any drunk, I was emotional rubble.

John slept well, ate well, entered and exited sleep with little fuss and no muss.

Samantha followed a different path. The NICU nurses called the issue "inconsolable crying."

In my diminished state of functioning, I called it a disaster. John would awaken, eat, return to sleep. Samantha would do this, too, and, at unpredictable intervals, she would cry. And cry.

To allow John—and my wife—to continue to sleep, I would take Samantha down to the family room and put her into the spare crib (once it became clear that holding her, walking her, rocking her, and begging wouldn't stop the wailing). I would rub her back then find my bathrobe.

In the middle of the night, the neighborhood lit unevenly by oddly spaced streetlights, I would step onto my porch, plant myself on the cold cement stairs, and cry.

I never mentioned this to my wife.

When Sam and I were done crying, I would return her to the office crib and return myself to the floor. Until the next feeding.

The days were better than the nights, but I wasn't.

Not knowing what I needed, I settled on Dr. Phil.

Hearing the hyperbolic traumas Phil's guests displayed put things into skewed perspective.

More importantly, I see now, Dr. Phil's appearance meant that my wife would be home in two hours. One hundred and twenty minutes.

Anyone who has a tattoo knows that everything can be managed for this amount of time, no matter how uncomfortable.

It wasn't about Dr. Phil. It wasn't about endless dirty diapers or too-rich formula mixtures or crying sorta drunken tears.

It was about routine. It was about being a father all night and day... and then getting a break.

I am the last of my branch of the family tree (until my kids put out some limbs of their own). So I've become the keeper of the relics. I have all of the old report cards, scrapbooks, photo albums, and newspaper clippings. Recently, as I went through a box of random remembrances, I came upon five copies of my sister's funeral program, a newspaper clipping that retold the story of my father's life being threatened by a well-armed drunk (Dad was a deputy at the time, walking into a domestic disturbance—that innocuous-sounding term that appears in the obituary of a lot of cops), and a short news story about a shooting that happened at my grandfather's gas station in Gardiner, Montana. I'd never heard a word about the shooting, not that I can remember. In this same box, I came upon maybe a dozen Mother's Day cards, some homemade, some store-bought, some from my sister, some from me. There wasn't a single Father's Day card. Not one. I have other boxes that I still haven't gone through. There won't be any Father's Day cards in any of them. I'm almost positive.

Dad's Here?
September/October 2007

I EXPECTED A lot of the things that happened when my twins, John and Samantha, were born. I expected to lose the pristine back seat of my sporty little car to child seats and spilled milk. I expected to lose my home office to a monster-sized crib. I expected to disappear from the lives of my childless friends for long stretches of time. I even expected to pay nearly half of my monthly salary for good, professional, full time daycare.

I never expected to have my feelings mauled regularly by those full time daycare providers, though.

Like most parents of twins and other multiples, my wife and I learned early that we can only manage our lives as a couple and a family if we divide every child-related chore equally—from feeding the kids to ferrying them around. Total equality.

As a father, however, I have noticed that a pervasive inequality exists: At daycare, the children craft things weekly, from paper flowers in Styrofoam vases to modern art abstractions in finger paint. Holidays such as Valentine's Day and Halloween involve both. All of this we-love-you artwork is for either their *mother* or their *parents*. None of it is for dad.

Mother's Day was a big deal at John and Sam's daycare. The kids made little booklets about their mommies. They made flower bouquets out of construction paper and popsicle sticks. They made big hearts with "Mom" written in red ink, tiny hand and foot prints all around.

It was all so cute that it brought tears to my eyes. Still does. I even framed some of it to hang in their mother's office.

I began looking forward to Father's Day, casually scanning the tables and shelves when I'd pick my twins up, on the lookout for ongoing artwork. In conversations with their teachers, I trolled for information about what to expect. I wondered how large a frame I'd need if I tried to include everything in my own office-wall display.

Father's Day came and went without a ripple. No flowers. No hearts. No construction paper, red ink and popsicle sticks. I was so sure that there'd been a mistake that I asked my wife to check, when she dropped the kids off, to see if I'd somehow missed my artwork.

I hadn't missed anything. There was nothing to miss.

"You ok?" my wife asked me when she called with the bad news.

"No," I replied. "This really hurts my feelings." That may be the least masculine thing I've ever said. It's also entirely accurate, and it's a feeling I would spare other fathers.

To deal with my artwork impoverished office, I stopped waiting for daycare to provide me with frame-worthy materials. A quick trip to a local super-center landed me large sheets of paper and big Crayons suitable for tiny hands. I bought finger paints and sponges for stamping. I added art-and-craft time to our after-dinner schedule.

My office now sports a steady stream of John and Sam originals. As a side benefit, the art that doesn't end up with me or my wife tends to move outward into the family, especially on birthdays and Grandparents' Day. Some of it, laminated at a local print shop, becomes placemats for the table.

This solution enlivened my office space, gave the extended family a nice connection to the kids, and added a fun ritual to our routine, but it did nothing to soothe my hurt feelings in relation to the daycare folks. Thankfully, my problem materialized just as new teachers and new management moved in to this local learning center.

So I've begun asking them questions long before every major holiday. What are the kids doing and when? Any supplies I can help out with? On a personal level, these questions and their answers make me an even more engaged participant in the daycare where my children spend the bulk of their time during the week. Possibly because I've been such a polite bother to them, the new management has begun sending home monthly calendars of activities, including art projects.

I'm optimistic about my chances next Father's Day.

My wife has been out of town for less than an hour...and I just spent a good bit of time explaining to four nine-year-olds how to more accurately shoot one another with some surprisingly powerful Nerf guns.

Most damning dialogue, when taken out of context: "John, the other crossbow is by the wagon."

My wife and I weren't paranoid, but we worked pretty hard at baby proofing the house from the very beginning. It helped that we had a huge green pillow, maybe seven feet long and two feet tall. We could lay that thing down diagonally and keep two crawlers away from the Christmas tree, no sweat. Keeping John and Sam safe in the kitchen was much more complicated. The "incident" involving John's hand and the oven door led to this, which is, I think, the first article I published about my kids.

On Twins and Kitchen Safety
July/August 2008

ELIZABETH AND I have twins who began walking well before their first birthday—and immediately walked into trouble, particularly in the kitchen. Because I cook the majority of our meals and my wife bakes frequently, the kitchen is a hub of activity. John and Samantha want to be near us, and being near us in the kitchen puts them in harm's way. We took all the usual precautions covered in baby-safety articles: a latch on the oven door, clips that hold drawers and cupboards closed, covers on the electrical outlets. It wasn't enough.

The accident happened when my wife was baking cookies.

Our son, who'd only learned to walk days before, saw the open oven door and rushed it. Before we could react, his tiny hand slapped flat onto the pre-heated surface. He began to scream. To howl.

I don't panic easily. I panic spectacularly.

Gathering John up in my arms, I ran for the bathroom, enacting a half-formed plan to get his hand under cold running water. Logically, it would have been both easier and quicker to use the kitchen sink, and not running headlong through the house might have kept him from panicking, too. It certainly would have added less drama to this unfolding trauma.

Ah, hindsight.

Instead of reacting logically, I grabbed, ran, and generally made a bad situation terrible. Worse, I have no memory of where Sam, John's twin sister, was during any of this. I'd been laying on the living room floor, lifting her above me and tickling her belly, when John screamed in pain. I guess I set her down, ran to the kitchen, etc. I guess. Presumably, she sat on the floor where I'd left her, not crying and not panicking while I (and my wife) did both.

Urgent Care dealt with the burn, while Tylenol handled the lingering pain. I dealt with the guilt, shame, and horror of what had happened by turning John's hand into a bandage-wrapped club—as if extra layers of dressing could undo his first trauma (our first as parents). Before I could trust the kitchen again, changes had to be made. None of them major. All of them significant.

Scribble on This

During graduate school I once rented an apartment where the bathroom walls had been covered by not wallpaper but contact paper—a gray granite sort of pattern. This paper had been applied over the original plaster—lumpy and crumbling—leaving the walls with a through-the-looking-glass sort of unevenness.

Since living in this apartment, I have carried an irrational dislike of contact paper—a dislike now erased by its usefulness in my kitchen. Specifically, after John's injury, I looked for ways to keep small hands busy and safe while keeping them close to me. I found contact paper that doubles as a chalkboard.

At the end of my kitchen cupboards and on the far side of the island, I pasted two sheets of this rough black paper. I bought sidewalk chalk—its size perfect for toddler hands and also slightly less likely to snap under pressure—and kept it in a tiny bucket in the nearest cupboard.

For less than ten dollars, I kept John and Sam occupied at a safe distance from the stove. We're still working on coloring only on the paper and not on the walls, floor, dog, or each other.

No Latches Here

No toddler can remain focused upon a single activity for long, and twins are no exception to this rule. The contact paper chalkboard worked as a place to start, but writing on a chalkboard is a single activity that grows stale in isolation. To keep things less monotonous, I emptied out the nearest cupboard—the furthest from the stove—and loaded it with toys. Noisy toys.

The cupboard acts as a safe place to store the chalk, but, like a simple cardboard box, its own lure is irresistible. So it's a safe place to store the twins, too. When not coloring with chalk or playing with those noisy toys—the bells and whistles help me keep track of the kids' location even with my back turned—John and Sam often crawl into the cupboard and close the door behind them. The door cracks open occasionally as I cook or wash dishes, mostly to emit a burst of dad-can't-find-us giggles.

There's not much storage in my kitchen, and the loss of a cupboard is hard to bear. But there are worse things to lose than cupboard space.

Don't Cross that Line

When I work around the home, I always buy more supplies than I need, assuming on some level that the extra material will come in handy later. As John and Sam colored on their chalkboard and played in their cupboard, I looked for a clear, visual cue to tell them where not to be while I cook. I needed a safety zone around the stove and between the stove and sink—the high-traffic cooking space.

The kitchen floor is a virtually unbroken, seamless expanse of linoleum, and the layout provides no obvious spatial divisions. Chalk lines rub off too easily, while inked lines don't rub off easily enough;

colored masking tape leaves glue splotches that must be peeled up. But the blue tape that remained from my last painting project solved this dilemma nicely.

As John and Sam watched, I stretched tape across the kitchen, "walling" off the most dangerous spaces and visibly separating them from the safe play region. Sitting crosslegged on the floor, I explained the Blue Line to them, repeatedly talking about cooking and kitchen safety and unwanted trips to the ER—all couched in terms such as "hot, hot" and "no, no." Sam gave me a dubious look (not the first she's ever offered when one of my plans is explained to her). John studiously crinkled his brows, possibly wondering if my absurdity, like my dimples, is genetic.

When the chalkboard gets boring and the cupboard isn't interesting, the Blue Line saves me. It took a surprisingly small number of "hot, hot" and "no, no" discussions for remaining outside the Line during meal preparation to become a habit.

Now I just need to give The Look or The Dramatic But Silent Finger Point to send an errant toddler scuttling back across the line to safety. Generally there's giggling, as it's become a contest to see who can cross the line in the tiniest way. Thus far, John's pinky finger extended just slightly beyond the tape is the record holder.

The Look and The Point, like the giggling and scuttling, are preferable to burns and panic and visits to the hospital.

There are pictures of John with his hand bandaged, and he's smiling in all of them. I smile now, too, as he and Sam help me cook—their help generally causing every kitchen-based activity to take three times longer. But the memory of a tiny hand slapped onto a hot oven door, the memory of a tiny scream, erases my smile still and makes my heart pound—not because of what happened but because of what could have happened.

So many things other than a little hand could have touched that oven door.

My kitchen is still a hub of activity, from auto races on the linoleum to epic GI Joe versus Spiderman grudge matches on the table.

My kitchen is a safer place than ever before, as John and Sam color with chalk, crawl in and out of their cupboard, and stay safely behind the blue line.

The Oven Door

If your oven is like mine, then the oven latch it already has (for the self-cleaning cycle) cannot be used during normal baking. While there are several varieties of latch available, none of them seem to have an adhesive attachment that can long survive normal wear-and-tear. To keep my latch in place, I used Gorilla Glue. This latch may now be a permanent part of the oven.

Knobs on the Stove

Generally, these slip over the peg on which the temperature control knobs for the stovetop rotate. They snap shut and can't be opened by little hands. But these same little hands can pull the entire apparatus off the stove, knob and cover combined. Use these until something better comes along. Then stop using them.

Drawer & Cupboard Latches

While there are many varieties of latches to hold drawers and cupboard doors shut, all of them are of a kind: one piece that connects to the wooden frame, another that connects to the door or drawer. Pull on the door/drawer and the latch engages; pull just a little and then reach in to push down on the latch and the latch doesn't engage. This simple safety measure works well to keep toddlers out of the knife drawer or cleanser storage cupboard. It takes a good amount of finger strength to push down on the latch. Of course, this means that elderly visitors, like my wife's grandparents, are also barred from grabbing a knife or a bottle of Windex.

First Aid Kit

Burns and cuts. These are the likely kitchen injuries, and the smaller, less severe of them can be handled with a bit of disinfectant cream, some kind of covering, and a kiss. Daddy kisses, however, are 27 percent less effective than Mommy kisses.

Vigilance

No latch or line on the floor substitutes for vigilance and good judgment. Use the burners on the back of the stove instead of always using the front. Don't run the TV or music if it means you'll pay less attention to the children. "Accidents happen," John often tells me when we discuss potty training issues. And accidents do happen, but some accidents can be avoided.

In 1993, I was interviewed by a fellow student during a day-one, get-to-know-you sort of activity in a teacher-training workshop (the sort of gathering that would, in another century and State, produce the beginning of "Shoot the Drift"). We worked from a set list of questions, all designed for folks making the transition from English student to English teacher. Decades later, I still remember the last question perfectly: "If you could write about anything, what would you pick?" When I was asked this, I responded immediately and without any sort of mental or emotional filter managing to intervene: "My sister," I said. "I'd like to write about my sister. She was killed in an accident when I was young." When the woman who interviewed me read this aloud, I happened to be looking right at my friend Dave. He heard my answer and briefly closed his eyes. He understood the gravitational pull one person can have on the orbit of a life. Still, this essay about my sister wasn't drafted until early in 2006. And it didn't see publication in Fourth Genre *until 2013, twenty years after my declaration of intent.*

Peter Benchley is Dead

The museums in children's minds, I think, automatically empty themselves in times of utmost horror—to protect the children from eternal grief.
— Kurt Vonnegut, *Slapstick or Lonesome No More!* (16)

I'M SCREAMING MYSELF awake, fighting against the light blanket and kicking at the dog. Sweat pours down the sides of my face and down my back. The sheets beneath me are wet, as is the pillowcase. I fell asleep watching *Jaws* on DVD, watching the 30th anniversary edition, and the theme song plays as Sheriff Brody fires wildly at the rapidly approaching shark. The DVD is new, a gift from my wife, but its effect on me is not.

When composer John Williams wrote this basically two-note tune, penned under the snappy name "Main Title and First Victim," he probably had no idea that this simple harmony would win part of the film's Oscar for Best Original Score. He couldn't know how deeply it would scar and scare both a tiny boy in Montana and an entire generation of movie-watching former swimmers.

For more than three decades it soundtracks my dreams.

I feel my heart beating in my wrists. My eyes throb. I'm not sure I've ever felt my heartbeat in such an obvious, almost painful way. I can hear a ringing in my ears. This all scares me in a middle-aged way I'm not ready for at this time of night.

I force my way out of the tangled sheets with rapid, angry motions and pad barefoot and bare-chested to the bathroom where I get a drink of water, using the purple cap from my shaving cream as a cup. The water won't get cold no matter how long I wait, so I drink three or four warm capfuls and go back to bed, slapping the television's "off" button as I pass.

My wife holds me: "What was it? Do you want to talk about it?"

I'm not sure if I've ever answered these linked questions, although she asks every time. I'm not sure if I'm going to answer now until I do: "It was Stacie. She was in my closet, and I could hear her calling my name. I knew she was dead."

I roll onto my stomach and try to think of something else. Of someone else. But it's dark, and I can still feel myself sweating, and the dream is very real.

I don't think about Stacie very often. I dream about her, though. Until now I never thought she scared me. Not after she was dead.

In the picture from Christmas morning, 1975, Stacie and I stand back to back, maybe a foot of space between us. We're both holding a newly opened present. Mine is a Tin Woodsman, a 12" action figure from *The Wizard of Oz*. He's mostly a gray blur in my hands, still wrapped in plastic. Stacie's got the best present of the day, however: a poster from the movie *Jaws*, one that shows the shark swimming directly at the viewer, tooth-filled mouth gaping. The poster's been unrolled like a large scroll, and she's displaying it for the camera—and looking over her own shoulder and down at me.

Stacie's almost eleven, while I'm only a few weeks into being five. We've both been obsessed with the movie *Jaws* since it opened the past summer. She loves *Jaws* and is utterly unafraid, willing to water-ski and fish at Georgetown Lake and to swim in any water without nervousness. Her bravery astounds me, and my own fears of water and the possibilities of violent death are put to rest in the shadow of her courage.

Once the presents are all opened, she'll have another poster, this one the lobby-print that shows the shark shooting straight upwards at the nubile young swimmer; a game simply called Jaws; and a vinyl record titled *Jaws of the Shark*.

Stacie and I listen to *Jaws of the Shark* constantly, turning off the lights and sitting close in the dark. The picture on the album cover shows a Great White swimming towards a diver in a cage. The shark's mouth looks large enough to swallow the cage whole.

With the red curtains on Stacie's bedroom window closed, the glow-in-the-dark vampire poster on her wall takes on a creepy, radiation-based light, greenish and unnerving. The record spins on her small stereo, pops and hisses drifting from the single speaker on the front of the plastic turntable's case.

The album takes maybe thirty minutes to twirl out in the dark, and we don't speak, don't interrupt the flow of the stories—stories of native islanders in canoes, divers in sunken Spanish galleons, stories of sharks. The main characters are a grandfather and his two grandchildren. Accompanied by Paul the deckhand, they roam an unnamed ocean doing some kind of research related to "Gramps'" work as a scientist.

In the dark, Stacie and I listen to *Jaws of the Shark* and stare at the album cover and feel the small thrill of fear. We know that the family will survive its terrifying adventures on and under the sea, but we fear for them any way.

In Stacie's Jaws game, the "board" is a plastic shark maybe a foot long, its mouth hinged to open wide and attached to a spring that snaps it closed. At the beginning of the game, the shark's mouth is filled with a handful of plastic items—a few white bones, a broken wagon wheel, a tire, a glove, etc. All things that could reasonably be found in a shark. Using a small plastic boathook, we take turns fishing items out of the shark's mouth. Eventually, one of us springs the shark's jaw, trapping the boathook and scattering any remaining plastic pieces everywhere. The loser is supposed to be the one to reset the game, snapping the mouth open and filling it with the pieces.

I lose a lot, but Stacie always helps me.

Peter Benchley's novel *Jaws*, originally titled *A Stillness in the Water*, was published in the winter of 1973-1974, roughly one and a half years before the film was released. By that year's Oscar Awards ceremony, nearly twelve million copies of *Jaws* were in circulation, not counting book club and Reader's Digest editions.

In 1975 my great grandmother can still read. It'll be almost five years before the cataracts blind her, and Stacie will be gone by then. While she can still read, she reads constantly. Reader's Digest sends the books every month without being asked, and once she is done reading all of them, she passes the books along to her daughter Alice, who passes them to my Aunt Kay. Each relative who reads a book writes her name on the inside front cover, often adding a one- or two-word critique. *Jaws* is, according to Alice, "fantastic." Eventually the books work their way back to Grandma Glasson, and she puts them on the small bookshelf in her living room.

Stacie and I don't find Reader's Digest's 1974 printing of *Jaws* until it's traveled out into the family and back again, some time after we've seen the movie. I can read by then, but not well. Not quickly, not aloud, and not with passion in the delivery.

Stacie can.

We sit together in my great grandfather's chair—a hideous rocking recliner covered in purple vinyl, the arms heavily repaired with layers of both silver duct tape and black electrician's tape—the book spread open upon our laps. Stacie reads with force while I follow along with my finger, running it beneath each word to mark her progress. As the tension builds in various scenes, she leans against me, pushing me into the corner where the back and armrest met. At truly exciting points, she makes sound effects: the beachfront screams of panic, the gurgles of swimmers pulled underneath the water, the booming explosion of a rifle.

I giggle a lot during these tense moments, but Stacie holds back her laughter to keep from spoiling the dramatization.

The pictures that accompany this abridged novel fascinate me, particularly the one that shows a diver in a cage, a huge shark forcing its way to him. The picture takes up an entire page, a cage hanging down on the left, a shark—shown only from nose tip to gill slits—arrowing in from the right. The shark has managed to pin its nose against the diver's belly, simultaneously crushing his torso and lifting his legs off the floor of the cage—propelling them toward a gaping mouth lined with teeth.

Once Stacie is gone, I return to this page in the novel, return to this picture, again and again. I rub my small fingers over the diver, the cage, the bubble-filled blue water. I don't touch the shark.

I hear Stacie reading.

My great grandfather's boat smells like a chemical spill. He mixes his fiberglass in ten-gallon batches, tattooed and scarred hands stirring the thick mixture, eyes watering from the industrial stink, and uses it for every repair, major and minor. Fresh repairs stink for days, like paint that's somehow gone rancid, while old patches—only sometimes smoothed with a trowel and sandpaper, crust and flake and leave dusty piles downwind of themselves.

The boat, a light pink when Johnson was still President, has a faded-out, piebald look, but it has power. Released into Georgetown Lake, it can pull a skier at a reckless, spray-throwing, wake-making speed that my seven-year-old's mind can't judge. The speedometer, which can't be fixed with fiberglass, has been broken for years.

Stacie, in cutoff jeans and a yellow KISS t-shirt mostly covered by her battered, grease-stained orange life jacket, flies over the water, cutting back and forth in rapid, showy curves that make her friends cheer wildly. Bobby and Robin have both had their turns at the end of the rope, and neither is as skilled as Stacie.

Chips steers his boat, an enormous man crammed into a small seat and hunched beneath the windshield's protective shadow. He drives with his left hand and holds the throttle with his right, which is two fingers short of a full complement and not nearly as strong. He rarely turns his head to look back, in deference to the speed, so we kids have to yell to him when each skier falls.

I sit in back with the teens but never even ask to ski. They'd let me, probably, but the thought doesn't enter my mind. Stacie's skill awes me, as does her absolute fearlessness. There could be anything under the water. Anything at all. Waiting to trip and bite or just to pull down and hold.

As Stacie executes another on-a-dime turn, she catches an edge and flips face first into the lake with a fwapping sound that's more visual than aural. She goes under, driven by her forward momentum, against which the lifejacket isn't strong enough.

I stand, begin looking for a fin. My heart pounds beneath my own lifejacket, yellow and cinched very tight. It smells like grease and dust and chafes a line across the back of my neck.

Chips hears the yelling and cuts the motor back, turning in a lazy arc to the left and bleeding off speed. I can see both skis floating in the boat's path, slowly drifting away from each other.

As we drift near the skis, Stacie's head breaks the surface, her face streaming water. She smiles at me, and I grin back with some effort. Her friends shout and laugh as they pull her in. I strain my eyes to look beneath the glare-bright water.

If I can't see the fin, maybe I can see the approaching shadow.

There aren't many pictures from Christmas day 1978, just a few of the presents being opened. Stacie isn't in any of the shots, and her absence is visible on my eight-year-old face. There are no shark-themed toys this year, but there are already nightmares, five months after her accident. Coming home from waterskiing at Georgetown Lake last summer, she fell from my great grandfather's pickup truck. The trailer carrying his boat passed over her body, crushing her chest. She died almost instantly.

My new train set, mounted on a large sheet of plywood, is always visible in the background of the '78 Christmas pictures, sometimes partially covered by a drift of wrapping paper and scatter of bows. Before all of the presents are unwrapped, I kneel on the edge of the plywood and cut my knee, a cut deep enough to reveal a wink of bone.

The cut is so sudden that the blood and pain don't immediately flow; I have time to look at what's happened and begin to evaluate the matter.

I shriek. Blood runs across the plywood, staining its clean, sanded-smooth surface. I've managed to kneel on the only edge that isn't entirely rounded. My father, twenty-nine years old and terrified, scoops me up and runs for the medicine cabinet, runs for the hydrogen peroxide and battered box of bandages. My mother, only months into being thirty, follows behind.

By the time I'm sitting on the closed toilet lid, sobbing, my leg is covered in blood like a sock. It takes all of our gauze and surgical tape to stop the bleeding, but by noon only two Ace bandages stretch across my knee. The X pattern they make seems very dramatic on my small leg.

When school resumes in 1979, I'll be in the dog days of second grade. I limp as the knee heals, scar tissue building one layer at a time, scabs forming and falling off. The scar is maybe a quarter of an inch wide, white and hairless and shaped like a frown.

It aches sometimes.

The news is on—what passes for news on CBS in the early morning—but I'm only listening with half an ear. The 2006 Winter Olympics in Torino, Italy, start soon, and there's some "women only" cruise going on, the kind of thing viewers wrote letters begging to get onto. These two stories, neither important, dominate the conversation I'm ignoring. Instead, I am feeding my son while his twin sister, Samantha, rolls on a blanket nearby, already fed and awash in her need to sleep.

We're sitting on the floor, facing each other, legs spraddled out to each side, the pose we sit in when we roll John's racquet ball back-and-forth. I'm tipping the bottle of milk upwards enough for him to suck at the rubber nipple. He's not eleven months old yet, but he can normally hold the bottle for himself. Today, he feels like having his father do the work.

A copy of *Jaws*—the Reader's Digest Condensed Version from 1974—rests on my bookshelf, only a yard from where we sit. Its cover is green and blue—a sort of floral pattern, like wallpaper in a grand-mother's living room—and I keep a yellow bookmark on the image where a caged diver meets his brutal end. The album *Jaws of the Shark* is on a high shelf, above the line-of-sight of my twins, already snugly dependent upon one another. Neither the book nor the album is a survivor of my childhood. Both are products of late night eBay searches and drunken bidding.

I keep a fossilized shark tooth on my desk, too. It runs almost three inches from tip to root, and I worry my thumb against it in anxious moments. I have to use care. After two million years of abrasive sleep at the bottom of the ocean, the edges are still serrated and slightly sharp to the touch. Once enamel white, the tooth has taken on the color of its geography and is brown from sitting for so long in shifting layers of sandy silt. The shark that hunted with this tooth was dead and gone while my Montana home still held a large part of the North American Inland Sea.

As John finishes his bottle, I hear something important rise from the television's palaver: Peter Benchley, author of the novel *Jaws*, the children's book *Jonathan Visits the White House*, and one-time speech-writer for President Lyndon Johnson, is dead. I don't hear anything that follows, don't hear any of the details of where and how and what the commentator thinks this writer's life meant.

I lean forward, reaching over Samantha's now sleeping body, and poke the television's on/off button. I pull my son into my lap and rock him, soothing myself with this rhythm.

It took "Peter Benchley is Dead" a long time to find a home,
but the waiting paid off: Fourth Genre *is a top journal in*
the field of creative nonfiction. The editor and reviewers just
hated the ending, though, and they wanted me to change it.
When my inner writer hears "change," he starts pounding
away. I just kept adding to the essay, somehow assuming
that I was going to write my way to a better ending. I didn't.
Eventually, I trimmed a few sentences from the original draft
that was accepted for publication, and everything fell into
place. That extra ending still makes me smile, though, and
I've included it here: "Peter Benchley is Dead" (draft ending).

At dinner last night—at Barclay II in Anaconda—Sam was
spelling "Montana" and using each letter as the beginning
of a word that describes the state. "M" was, of course, for
"Mountains." "A" stood for "Angry." John asked what she
was doing and pointed out that "angry" wasn't the same
sort of descriptive word as the others. Sam explained: "The
weather is 'angry.' I was using personification." (Imagine that
last sentence spoken in the most snooty voice a nine year
old can level on her brother.)

*After my great grandfather committed suicide, his widow
married her son's cellmate. I've written pieces of the story,
but the first writing I ever did was about the great grandfather
who was there in my childhood, Charles Glasson ("Chips"
to everyone, although no one knows why). In an essay in*
Conclave, *titled "Chips," I told the story of his criminal history, which began at a reformatory in Idaho and extended
across state lines for decades. It's a good story, in a bad way,
one that begins with "theft of a horse" and ends with the rape
of a child. The real story, though, is about the tension that
develops while loving someone who probably didn't deserve
it. If that conflicted sort of love's a question, then I don't have
an answer. Instead, I have an Icky Papa, to use the name
John and Samantha applied to Chips.*

Icky Papa Died
2008

I WAS RELIEVED when my great grandfather died. I learned of
the event more than a year after the fact, simultaneously ingesting
the information that he'd passed in Idaho, that he'd been buried in
Montana, and that his grave—while next to my great grandmother's—
was unmarked and expected to remain that way. No one in Idaho
wanted him buried there, and no one in either state would spring
for a tombstone.

A horse-thief-turned-burglar-turned-forger-turned-rapist probably
can't expect much better, even if he is family.

The last time I saw him I was twelve, and he was standing stolidly
in the white-gravel of his driveway and asking, "Are you mad at me?
Because your mother sure is." He was remarrying. No one was anything but mad at him. I nodded my answer, dropping an armload of
brightly colored books into the trunk of my parents' red Volkswagen.

Almost thirty years after I nodded my answer, I discovered Chips' prison records from 1937. "His picture," I say over dinner and around a mouthful of steamed broccoli, "was right on top of the file. It didn't look anything like him, didn't look anything like the guy in all the other mug shots even."

Elizabeth shrugs and doesn't point out that the picture is of a thin boy who just turned eighteen, while the great grandfather I remember was sixty-five and fat and remarrying and liked to push his thumb into the bottom of pieces of chocolate to get a glimpse of the filling. When he was finished, there'd be a sweet-smelling cardboard container staffed by a random smattering of violated candies that no one would eat.

John is three and sits to my left at meals. He knows I'm going to make him eat broccoli before he can leave the table. Now, as I speak of my great grandfather's long criminal record, John furrows his brow and asks, "What papa?"

This is a simple grammatical structure for a complicated question: I chew and consider my range of possible answers. John still hasn't grasped that my father is his grandfather, so this discussion of Chips is already on some shaky ground. Too much abstract genealogy.

Elizabeth steps in to save me from the place I've talked myself into: "This papa died a long time ago, John."

He looks from his mother to me. "He got dead?" I nod and eat more broccoli. Because I'm an English teacher, I almost never correct my son's grammar, even when it'd be a good way to change the subject. John immediately shares his new knowledge across the table with his twin sister: "Hey, Sam!" This comes at full volume, John leaning from side to side to see around the collection of salts and spices that serve us as a centerpiece. "Sam! The Icky Papa died!"

I notice that "got dead" has become "died," which is good. Chips has also gone immediately from being an abstraction to being an icky, which is both hard to understand and hard to correct. Chips *was* icky. Still, my instinct is to defend him—or at least to correct my son's rudeness.

"Honey," I normally would say, "We don't call people icky. That's not nice." But I can't correct him here because he's right and because I'm the great grandson who smiled when he learned that Chips was dead.

"Honey, eat your broccoli. That's all that's standing between you and dessert."

At bedtime, John's serious, not even singing the ABC song. I tell him the story of Terry Troll, resident bridge builder in my Kingdom of NeverEverWas, and he doesn't interrupt. As I begin to leave, he stops me: "Daddy? The Icky Papa died?" His voice is filled with innocent anguish that hurts me deep in my chest, hurts me in a scary, middle-aged way I'm not ready for.

"Yeah." My knees both pop loudly as I stand.

"Were you mad?"

His question freezes me, sends a spider down my spine. "No, John, I wasn't mad."

My answer satisfies him, at least. John rolls to his side, faces the wall, falls asleep with his arm over the battered orange and green cover of *Go Dog Go*. I watch him breathe, my mouth dry, my feet planted solidly on the graying bedroom carpet.

> *My family moved to Fernley, Nevada, in 2005. We had no reason to live in Fernley and no love for the place. Our first night there, someone broke into the garage and stole a random box of unpacked stuff. I'm still not sure what went missing—maybe a box of professional journals that would have ended up in my office, maybe cleaning supplies. Definitely our sense of security. That burglar made nothing off the theft from my garage; ADT Security should have paid him a commission, since I called them the next morning. We ended up in Fernley because the housing market was wildly inflated in Reno. Even in Fernley, we paid $253,000 for a home half the size of our home in Washington (which we had built). The housing bubble burst, and when we left Nevada for Montana, that $253,000 home sold for $65,000. I had a big list of home improvements for the realtor to go*

over—everything I'd done, from painting inside and out to landscaping the once-barren backyard. She couldn't have cared less, not at that price. All that mattered to me about that home, in the end, was the bedroom the kids shared (which became John's bedroom, once they were separated). Once the U-Hauls were packed, I walked into that room and stood in the corner, stood in the place where a rocking chair used to be. It's where I sat to read to the kids every night, night after night. I put my hands against the wall—"buttered popcorn" colored, according to the paint bucket from Ace Hardware—and rubbed the knock-down texture. I cried a little, not because we were leaving but because John and Sam would never be in that room again, that room where I once stood and declared my lack of anger toward my great grandfather. I never told anyone about those tears, and neither my father nor my father-in-law noticed that I was inside for a few extra minutes in John's bedroom.

There are moments I'll never forget. That's what I tell myself when they happen. And some of them do stick: When my son stepped into the backyard for the first time, I saw the wind hit him in the face, something he'd never felt before. I saw him blink. I saw the shock. He couldn't possibly remember that, but I do. Most of the moments I think I'll never forget are... just forgotten. Sometimes, I come across a piece of writing, though, that brings it all home again. "On Being Thankful" is one of those misplaced memories that's come home. It was written during the most painful year of my professional life, a year when I decided to leave academe entirely. I gave away most of my books, some office furniture, a homemade hutch that perfectly fit the desks everyone in the English Department at UNR used. Obviously I didn't leave for long, but I only came back when I found a job that was true to who I really am—and locates my family in a place only two hours (less, really) from where I grew up. This essay was originally written, I think, for Twinslink, a web site that doesn't seem to exist anymore.

On Being Thankful
2009

MY SON STANDS at the edge of the canal, cocooned in a hand-me-down parka and prying rocks out of the frozen ground. Holding each rock in his mittened hands, he toddles to the edge of the bank, rears back, and lobs the stone in a wobbly arc to the water below. The skin of ice is paper thin, and each rock smacks through with a brittle snap.

After every throw John looks back at me and grins in a way that hurts my heart. His sister is still napping. Elizabeth is baking, listening to *A Carpenter's Christmas*, listening for Samantha to wake up. I'm with John, at the canal, giving an ill-conceived lesson in rock throwing. "Careful," I say every now and then. The parka makes him top-heavy. When he leans over to dig ammunition, John almost always loses his balance. He keeps catching it, but I know that's mostly luck. "Careful."

The water isn't deep and isn't moving fast. The fall wouldn't be far, only three feet, and I could pull him out before he could drown. We're only two blocks from home. I can run that far, even carrying a wet child.

There's no danger here, but I can't stop sweating. I stand behind my son and watch him throw rocks. My hands, rolled into painful fists, are jammed into my jeans. The joy John takes in throwing rocks through the thin ice is pure and uncomplicated and beautiful, and I have to stop him.

I'm shaking with my desire to stop him.

"Careful," I say a few more times, almost hyperventilating with anxiety so out of proportion with what's happening that it's alarming. Finally, I convince him to walk home using the inducement of freshly baked cookies. I stop sweating and shaking as we walk, but I can't stop thinking, can't stop picturing my son—in no danger and perfectly happy—throwing rocks into the icy canal that dead-ends our street.

I think about this for days. As I'm watching the news, teaching my classes, driving to work. John throwing rocks into the canal. More, I think about the undiluted joy he took in this act. Nothing complicated, nothing multilayered: Dig a rock, rear back, throw and listen to the ice smash.

I stood in the dark hallway, warm in Seattle's June heat, listening to John and Sam carry on their first extended (and private) conversation. They were four, were on vacation, were sharing a room for the first time since early infancy. Their grandparents were asleep upstairs, and the cousins had gone home. My wife was asleep down the hall, in the room she denned in as a teen. Stumbling through the darkness, because I neither knew the way in the dark nor where to find the light switches, I stopped outside their bedroom door. I had to, when I heard the conversation:

"Are you talking about Batman?" John sounded confused, maybe even exasperated.

"No." Sam is often Spartan in her responses.

"He wears a mask but is blue and is tough?"

"Yes, right."

"I think you mean Subzero."

I smiled to myself. They'd watched me play an Xbox 360 game involving DC Comics characters versus the traditional Mortal Kombat combatants several weeks before we began to vacation our way through the Pacific Northwest, and apparently the game had made an impression.

It was quiet for a time, and I could easily picture my blonde toddlers laying flat on their backs, John on the bottom bunk and Sam on the top, mulling things over. "Do you think," Sam began, "that he's tougher?" I leaned closer to the door, smiling. This was a living flashback to every conversation I had between seven and seventeen: who is tougher than whom? I was trying not to laugh.

"Who," John asked, "Subzero?"

"Yeah, is he stronger than Daddy?" The tone of her voice suggested that Sam thought that I could, in fact, take him.

I nearly burst into tears. Which wouldn't have helped my stats any, I'm sure, in the matchup of Daddy vs. Subzero. John and Sam never did work this out, shifting to talk of spiders, *The Chronicles of Narnia*, and swimming in places that had waterslides (which they'd recently done for the first time). Standing outside their shared bedroom, the only other person to be awake in the house, I could feel my heart pounding, feel the aching lump in the back of my throat, feel my concerns over money and work and friends in the National Guard slide briefly away.

I feel strangely ambivalent about Thanksgiving and Christmas. Not in a Grinchy sort of way or a Peppermint-Patty-Throwing-a-Fit-at-Charlie-Brown sort of way, though. For two months or more, we're all told not only when to be thankful but what to be thankful for. Join hands around the table, every movie and sitcom and random holiday-themed commercial argues, and give thanks for family and friends and the fact of being together.

I *am* thankful for these realities in my life, of course. Family matters. Friends matter.

But I feel strange, and I don't think I'm alone in this, because being told what to be thankful for makes it just a little harder to remember the chance moments of joy and random acts of gentleness that make life especially wonderful.

I am thankful for the image of John's small hands, covered by mittens, pulling rocks from the ground and tossing them awkwardly into the canal.

I am thankful that my daughter believes me to be tough and that she and her brother already, at four, show clear and consistent fondness and love for each other.

These are the moments that matter to me in my definition of myself as a father and in my emotional foundation as a parent.

And for the record, I think I can take Subzero, too.

I keep terrible records. Terrible. I've managed to work out a system that keeps my tax receipts straight, but my writing is...messy. This article on depression was, in one Word file, clearly labeled: word count, sidebar word count, etc. All the information an editor would need. But there's nothing about where it was published, when, or by whom. Google comes up with nothing. If I had to guess, and apparently I do, then I'd say that this was the last article I wrote for one parenting magazine; their editorial staff changed, and suddenly I couldn't seem to get anyone to send me the money we'd agreed on. So maybe this article comes out of that mess. Maybe it was published, but I never received a complimentary copy. I'm at a loss.

Struggling in Silence: Parenting and Postpartum Depression

I COME OUT of a scratchy, shallow sleep—the only sort of sleep I can manage between the midnight and three o'clock feedings. Samantha is crying. Shrieking. I have to do something about it before she can wake her twin brother, John. Not even three months old, they still share a crib, just as they did for a month in the neo-natal intensive care unit.

I'm still dressed in my jeans and t-shirt, so rolling out of bed and onto my feet takes no time at all. I lift Sam's swaddled body and gently cradle her against my shoulder. Her inconsolable sobbing tears a hole in my heart as her tiny fists flail away at my face. We walk in long, aimless circles through the dark house, but she continues to wail. We rock in the wooden chair by the window, watching occasional cars flash past, running the stop sign at our corner. We rock in the plush recliner by the fireplace, now grown shadowy and cold.

Sam cries across both of these activities, walking and rocking, so I give up. I gently lay Sam, still shrieking, in the portable crib that sits in our family room, and I return to the recliner. After another ten minutes of continual crying, I leave her alone—out of the recliner, up the stairs to the living room, out the front door and onto the cold concrete of the front porch. The door slams behind me, sounding very loud against this quiet neighborhood night. Even through two inches of solid-core door, I can hear Sam. If I still smoked cigarettes, then this would be the time to light up. If I still drank, then this would be the ideal time to pop a cold beer. Instead of smoking and drinking, I wrap my arms around my folded knees, listen to my daughter cry, and burst into tears. In a brief but poignant moment of clarity between my own sobs, I realize that I am a mess. I even say this aloud in the dark night: "I am a mess."

And I've been a mess ever since my twins were born.

The IVF process was freakishly painless, physically, emotionally, and economically. After meeting with the doctor, my spouse and I met with the in-house financial planner. We talked about $12,000 as if it were nothing abnormal, even though the Ford I'd just purchased actually cost less, and my Ford was under warranty and thus guaranteed to work. We talked about donor eggs, the possibility of low sperm counts and ways to remedy this. The talk seemed endless, a long and detailed description of various hopeful scenarios, all seasoned with generous pinches of "however" and "if-this-then-that" rhetoric.

And all this talk ultimately seemed pointless: We did the IVF procedure, and nearly three dozen donor eggs were successfully fertilized. Only two were implanted, and both immediately attached themselves and began to do all the right things that viable embryos do. As the pregnancy progressed, gestational diabetes landed out-of-the-blue, but a few tweaks to our diet seemed to handle the problem nicely. Six weeks of full bed rest culminated in early labor, but the kids were healthy and fully developed—no lung issues, eye issues, or any of the other terrifying preemie problems that can occur when babies aren't carried to full term. John and Sam spent four weeks in the hospital, mostly learning the rhythm of suck-swallow-breathe.

All of these problems and potential problems came and went, and we were no worse for the wear.

After John and Sam were born and before they even came home, however, parenthood hit me like a punch in the dark. I cried quite often and felt hopeless and helpless even more often. I rarely slept, barely ate, and snapped irritably at every adult around me. I had headaches and spent hours on the couch—not reading or watching TV but just lying down and feeling bad and bullied by life and dumb for bringing this all on myself. It was post-partum depression in every conceivable form, and it should have been simple enough even for the people around me to diagnose, but neither they nor my doctor saw the problem for what it was.

Of course, no one was looking for post-partum depression in me, since I'm a father and not a mother.

I was irritated and angry, but no one thought it odd for a man to be this way. I was leaving a bad job and moving to a good one, which meant that while my wife was on full bed rest, I was packing boxes and renting a truck and working with our realtor to sell one house and buy another. The house we were leaving was only three years old; the house we were buying was thirteen years old, small, and almost twice as expensive. The textbook I was finishing was limping through a major revision, and all of my other writing projects had stalled entirely.

Of course I was depressed. What man wouldn't be upset—and maybe drink too much—with any one of these things going on? Add a high-risk pregnancy to the mix and the birth of twins, and depression is even more likely. It's expected. People would have been surprised if I wasn't depressed, irritable, angry, drinking too much and not sleeping enough. This casual cultural ignorance almost killed me. I was never suicidal, but that was just a fluke of my generally loving and upbeat temperament coupled with an overwhelming sense of love for my family. Things could have been different. Things very easily could have been different.

Almost four years after that night when Samantha and I both broke down and cried, Sam and I are watching television together. I'm stretched out on my bed watching *Meet the Press*, and Sam's enacting a dramatic solo version of *Five Little Monkey Jumping on the Bed*. Tom Brokaw appears on screen, and she stops: "What's his name?"

This is a sort of game we play. She asks me the names of everyone who appears on television, and I do my best to answer her, even if it means lying in a way that'll lead to giggles: "Who's that," I might say, "Why, that's Fumple Rumpdumpkin." Say this with enough shock in your voice and it gets a laugh out of any toddler. This time when she asks, however, I don't have to lie for a laugh. I know the name: "That's Tom. He's nice."

Sam always likes to be reassured that the people on TV are nice.

She considers this for a minute, maybe waiting to see if I'm going to mention Fumple Rumpdumpkin. When I don't add more to my answer, she blurts out "Hey, he looks just like you!"

This gives me pause. Tom Brokaw is white and wears a suit to work, but that's about the end of what we have in common. He's older than my parents. Stupidly, I ask how I'm like Tom. With the total and unflattering honesty that only a toddler can manage, Sam patiently explains to me that, like Tom Brokaw, I have gray hair.

I'm 38 years old and still wear the mullet that I perfected in high school. I emphatically deny having any gray hair, so Sam begins to point. "Gray here," she says touching my left temple, "and here" at the front, directly above my right eye. "And here." She wiggles a finger through the beard on my chin.

We both laugh, and she goes back to jumping, but I can't pay attention to *Meet the Press*. Instead, I'm struck by how much fatherhood has changed me. I still wear the hair that'd be appropriate for a man much younger, but I've left behind all of the other habits from that time in my life. Smoking. Drinking. Fun with my friends at all hours of the night, mostly involving smoking and drinking.

Becoming a parent cut me off from that life, a life where friends and I could watch football in a crowded bar virtually non-stop from Sunday morning through Monday night. A life where my wife and I could just walk into a bookstore and browse for two hours, or sit on the floor and eat crab legs while watching *Goodfellas*, or any number of things that stop being possible when a couple becomes a family. Thank God.

All of this self-centered and selfish living went away in the instant John and Sam were born, but it didn't go without a fight. As a new father, I couldn't be the man I'd been for all of my adult life, and I wasn't yet ready to be a father, wasn't ready to step into those big shoes. For centuries women have known about the Baby Blues, and for decades medical science has understood post-partum depression (in women). With centuries of "toughen up ya baby" sentiment pushing down on me, I had nowhere to turn but in, and there wasn't any help inside me.

I would spare other fathers this experience, but studies suggest that at least 10 percent won't be spared at all, while only slightly more women will suffer.

I can laugh now when Sam points out my gray hair. And she's right: There is gray hair on my temple, above my eye, and in my beard. It's funny now. Three years back, nothing was funny about being a father.

On Men and Depression

No one wants to hear how hard it is to be a man. Men make more money than women and have fewer doors closed—and far more opened—because of their gender. White men really have nothing to complain about, argues American culture at-large, especially when they are educated and employed.

No one wants to hear how hard it is to be a man, so men generally don't talk about it, even with other men. Instead, fatherhood hits—or mid-life is reached—and we disconnect from the life we've built, a life in which we suddenly feel simultaneously less important as ourselves and more like a walking source of income for those who depend on us. We drink. We cheat. We make excuses for drinking and cheating. We sometimes stop caring about anything, including ourselves. We become figures of ridicule as we buy new cars and clothes and the music of a generation half our age.

We commit suicide—or die of stress-related illnesses—at an alarming rate.

The names psychologists apply to us and to our problems hurt more than they help: IMS (Irritable Male Syndrome) sounds like something to describe the old guy on the corner who screams at kids to get off his lawn. Manopause just sounds like selfishness and self-centeredness masquerading as a pseudo-medical condition, although some evidence does suggest that the bodies of men go through a process similar in purpose but different in kind to the changes women experience in menopause.

Disease cuts across gender lines, and a condition such as breast cancer spares neither men nor women. But post-partum depression behaves in the same gender-neutral way. Watch new fathers, especially the fathers of multiples (who are even more likely to be sufferers). Don't trust to luck to pull them out of their downward spiral. Not all of us are lucky.

I might have mentioned how much I hated Nevada in general and Fernley, Nevada, in particular. When we moved to Fernley, there wasn't much there. In the course of five years, Walmart and Lowes came to town, along with half a dozen fast-food joints. Once the economy went to hell, the check cashing/payday loan places rolled in, too. We even had a place that specialized in giving loans that consolidated payday loans. At one point, I realized just how empty my street had become. It reminded me of my first Montana home. I told this story in the Fernley newspaper, and I've related a similar (condensed) version in the introduction to my third writing textbook, The Cost of Business.

Not Far from Montana
2010

MY FAMILY MOVED to Fernley in 2005, but, really, I've lived here all my life. I never expected to leave Montana in my teens and find myself home in northern Nevada in middle age, but the economy has forced this strange sense of homecoming upon me.

Anaconda, Montana, my hometown, was the child of the Anaconda Company, one of the primary players in the environmentally unsound copper mining boom of the late 1800s. Marcus Daly and the other copper kings dug their mines and imported the workers to keep them running—Irish, Italian, and German immigrants, mostly. Butte's "Richest Hill on Earth" became one of the largest copper-producing sites in the world. Much later it became the most polluted open pit on the planet, not counting Chernobyl in the former Soviet Union. Butte copper was smelted in Anaconda, and my father, my grandfather, and my great-grandfather worked at this smelter—sometimes after years spent deep in the mines themselves. The jobs were hard, of course, but they were also steady and sure and offered some overtime and room for advancement.

The best jobs in Anaconda were, without any doubt, at the smelter.

When the smelter closed in 1980, Anaconda lapsed into an economic coma. The smelter stopped giving out its dependable pay-checks, and suddenly there was less money being spent at the Washoe Theatre, the bars along Main Street and 3rd Street, the grocery stores. Bartending and cashiering jobs went from full- to part-time, while the lines got shorter at the grocery stores and longer at the churches that dispensed government commodities—welfare food—like rice and cheese. Families moved on, and classes got smaller in the schools, sometimes to the point that an entire school wasn't needed anymore.

I attended Beaver Dam Elementary—literally across the street from my home in a suburb named, without irony, Opportunity—until the Anaconda Company closed its Anaconda smelting plant. Once Beaver Dam closed its doors, I had to catch a bus that would take me ten miles to another school, the only elementary school left in town. The playground behind my closed school fell into a state of vandalized disrepair, and weeds overtook the baseball diamond. The high school, formerly housed in two enormous WPA-era buildings, was reduced to a single building, and even that survivor was sparsely populated.

It was like watching a town suffer through the late stages of some economic cancer that wasn't diagnosed until it had metastasized out of control. From 1980 to 1990, as much as 20 percent of the population would leave Anaconda—for jobs already secured, for the promise of jobs, or simply because there was no reason left to stay.

In this cancerous time, the best jobs that remained were at the prison in Deer Lodge or the mental hospital at Warm Springs, where one of my uncles had an inmate's thumb jammed into his eye all the way to the knuckle. Men who could get these jobs took them. Men who could retire did. Some men found jobs at the Hanford nuclear site in Washington. These jobs were often even better than what they'd done before, although the dangers were equally daunting—radiation poi-soning, rather than asbestos-caused cancer or an industrial accident. Eventually, my father would work security at Hanford, competing with men years younger than himself, before working his way into management. But that work in Washington would come later, after he spent long years working as a welder and pipefitter in places like Colstrip, Montana, and Pocatello, Idaho.

When the smelter closed, the men working there—and their families—did not understand the reasons. Looking back from 2010, the causes are clear and unavoidable and distant from western Montana. The causes, in fact, can be found in Asia and Latin America. In the late 1970s and early 1980s, Japanese copper flooded the world market, driving the price to sixty cents per pound. It was suddenly cheaper to buy internationally than to mine domestically. This radical market fluctuation was especially devastating to the Anaconda Company, which lost roughly 70 percent of its production capability in 1971, when newly inaugurated President Salvador Allende ordered all foreign-owned copper mines seized in the name of the Chilean people. These distant economic realities in Chile and Japan sent shockwaves through western Montana. They caused the ultimate collapse of the world copper market. They stripped my hometown of its only viable industry.

Even twenty years later, in 2000, the population of Anaconda remained at a level beneath that of 1980. More tellingly, the unemployment rate stood at nearly 10 percent, with the vast majority of employed workers in the service industry. The town has only slowly awakened from its economic coma—in a way that draws major industry, steady jobs, opportunities for growth and causes for hope. But it has begun to stir, as everything from new fast food to new professional golf courses appear across the landscape.

I left in 1989, for seasonal work in Yellowstone Park and then college classes in eastern Washington. For almost five years now, I've lived in Fernley, and I feel like Anaconda followed me, despite my best efforts.

Two years ago, just after I dropped my twins off at daycare one Monday morning, I saw my first foreclosure sign—right there, at the edge of an overgrown lawn, not too far from the 7-11. I looked away fast, like I was trying not to make eye contact with this public announcement that someone had defaulted on their mortgage. It scared me. It still scares me.

I work fulltime in Reno. My wife works fulltime in Fernley. Even with two incomes, we walk a financial tightrope—with mortgage payments, student-loan payments, credit card payments, and all the other bills that must be paid. Every ten days or so, I sit at my kitchen table and consider what to pay when. I count backwards from due dates to decide when a check goes in the mail. I look repeatedly at the calendar where I keep track of the payday schedule: While I only get paid at the end of each month, we're saved by my wife's bi-weekly checks. A few bills get paid online, but mostly I write checks. I can keep track of checks better, maybe because I'm not quite young enough to be part of the online generation that expects paperless bills and email alerts. There are nearly infinite details to keep track of, while still managing, with my wife, a household and the demands of parenting toddlers.

In the back of my mind, at every moment, I know that if I lose sight of a detail, then this financial juggling act crashes down—leaving me with a problem I can't afford: A bounced check, a lapsed insurance policy, a utility that gets turned off. I avoid these things consistently but narrowly, and the worry is always there, especially as I watch the value of my home shrink, despite my near-constant efforts to improve it—meticulously maintaining the yard, painting inside and out, wiring new light fixtures. There's no reason for me to take my home's loss of value personally, but I do.

It was this house that brought my family to Fernley in the first place, of course. We couldn't afford to buy in Reno, not in 2005, and now we can't afford to sell. Part of its decreased value is, naturally, just a feature of the Great Recession, but that's not all of it. Last year at this time, there were two houses at the end of my short street that were in foreclosure. At any given time, now, as many as five are actively for sale and/or are being rented. Last year at this time, I wasn't even the only UNR professor on my street. There were three of us. But both of the archaeologists who lived on the corner are gone now, early victims of the still ongoing layoffs in higher education in Nevada, and I'm one of the few actual homeowners left.

The small details keep reminding me that things are not ok for anyone in Fernley, really, any more than they were ok in Anaconda in 1980. This morning, as I drove to work in my Ford that gets more worn down every year but which I can't replace, another For Sale sign appeared on Main Street—representing another small business that couldn't make it any more. The building next door has been for sale for more than a year—another failed small business.

But it's also the small details that keep reminding me of better times to come.

The daycare my children attended for the first two years we lived in Fernley closed, but by then a number of larger and more professional daycares had opened. There are more jobs in the kid-care business in Fernley now than there were. WigWam closed about the time Black Bear Diner moved in, but the WigWam is open again. Amazon.com is still a major local employer, and it has been joined by Big Box giants like Lowes and Wal-Mart.

These are hard times in Lyon County generally and Fernley specifically, but hard times end.

I started publishing in the small press—while it still existed—in 1990 or 1991, so by the time I began to teach college-level writing in 1993, I felt like I had a little credibility. I'd team-taught maybe four literature classes and successfully taught 8th and 9th grade language arts for ten weeks at a less-than-top-shelf junior high. The amount of mentoring I received was...weak. My master teacher was pleasant and offered me support when I needed it, but I was a reward for hard work she'd done in some administrative post the year before. I was the school's way of giving her a paid vacation, so for ten weeks I taught everything from Poe to Harper Lee, from "The Pearl" to High Noon. *During that time, she sat in the teachers' lounge, eating popcorn and reading the newspaper. I still remember my first moments in the college-classroom clearly: I wore gray slacks and a sweater, and as I distributed the syllabus, I said (like a man fumbling his way through his first AA meeting), "I'm Shane Borrowman, and I'm nervous." But all of this is a long way of saying that for me, writing and teaching have virtually always gone hand in hand. Occasionally, that pairing leads to a pedagogical and personal essay like this, first published in* Brevity's *section of "craft" essays.*

Of Nails, Nonfiction & Various Adhesives
2006

MY FATHER STANDS behind me, watching and sweating in the Nevada sun. August is the worst possible time for roofing, but it's the only time we have. With the temperature hovering around one hundred, I'm on my knees, hammer in hand, about to be taught a lesson in writing creative nonfiction.

I take a couple whacks at the nails, hitting every time but not accomplishing much. Each nail takes three or four blows, and my shoulder is already stiffening.

"Choke back on the handle," my father says, his tone giving this piece of instruction just enough levity to lighten the sting. I'm sensitive about criticism, especially when it's criticism over something as simple as driving a nail, which I am clearly doing wrong.

I slide my hand back on the handle, and the next smack drives a fresh nail all the way through the shingles and into the plywood beneath.

I scoot to the side a bit, line up again, begin driving the next nail.

"Choke back," my father says again, and I realize that I've reverted to driving nails in my traditional, inefficient, painful-to-the-shoulder way. "Who taught you to hammer?"

"No one," I say, beginning to pound correctly. He doesn't answer, and I realize that I've hurt him. My answer slipped out, wasn't meant as a dig, can't be taken back. So I don't say anything else. Neither does he. The silence stretches out between us, punctuated only by the sound of hammering and the beat of the sun on our necks.

When I finish nailing the final row of shingles, my father holds the ladder as I climb down, hammer in one hand and bag of nails in the other. The knees of my jeans are black from shingle tar.

I haul everything into the stiflingly hot, dusty-stuffy garage, glad to be out of the sun. The temperature is well over a hundred in this enclosed, uninsulated space, but it feels wonderfully shady.

The hammer hangs above my workbench, suspended with its head across two metal pegs. The ladder is suspended from two hooks twisted deep into rafters, both sheathed in red rubber to give them a better grip.

The bag of nails, soft from sweat and handling and tar-sticky on the bottom, goes on a shelf filled with similar bags of dissimilar-sized nails.

Every tool and tool accessory in the garage has its place, and the floor glows in the dim light because of repeated sweepings. The cleanliness of this workspace is absurd and out of place, and it speaks ill of my mental health.

Behind the bags of nails is a long line of adhesives, arranged from weakest to strongest. A tiny bottle of Elmers hunkers meekly at the left, next to a varnish stained tube of wood glue. A double-barreled syringe filled with the components of epoxy lays before my Gorilla Glue, its cap sealed in place so solidly that I use pliers to open the squeeze bottle.

This is the adhesive collection of a man prepared for any contingency.

This is the adhesive collection of a man who rarely knows what he's doing or what he's going to need, a man willing to sometimes force connections.

Writing creative nonfiction requires a knack for linking lived experience with echoes of interpretation. It's all about carpentry, about nailing the pieces of narrative together with transitions, about spiking the past to the present to clarify both, about gluing surface events together to add strength and depth and meaning.

Some incidents go together easily, especially those that repeat across the years: Something happens; it reminds the writer of something that happened before. One event opens the story while the other gives it some closure. The events themselves are unrelated but not unlike one another. A little glue does the job.

Some incidents fit together badly, or not at all, until a few metaphorical hammer-whacks force the moments to their crises: Something happens, and both its causes and effects are unclear. Something else happens that seems unrelated. Whack. The "somethings" come together and stick after a pounding from the forces of passing time and research.

I never learned to drive a nail because of Latin American socialism and Asian mining practices.

In the late 1970s and early 1980s, Japanese copper flooded the world market, driving the price to sixty cents per pound. It was suddenly cheaper to buy internationally than to mine domestically. This radical market fluctuation was especially devastating to the Anaconda Company, which had lost roughly 70 percent of its production capability in 1971, when newly inaugurated President Salvador Allende ordered all foreign-owned copper mines seized in the name of the Chilean people. These distant economic quakes in Chile and Japan sent shockwaves through western Montana.

The mines in Butte—dubbed The Richest Hill on Earth—closed after more than a century of operation, leaving an open pit that would become one of the most toxically polluted points outside the former Soviet Union.

The smelter in Anaconda, twenty-one miles away and entirely dependent on Butte-mined copper, closed.

Suddenly my father, like virtually every man in town, was cast as the central character in a song by John Cougar Mellencamp.

Or possibly Bruce Springsteen.

Some of my friends' fathers took work as guards at either the state prison in Deer Lodge or the mental hospital at Warm Springs. Several found work at the Hanford nuclear site in Washington. Others, my father among them, found work at construction sites in eastern Montana and the Dakotas—union work that paid well but kept them from home for months at a stretch when the roads were bad due to weather.

Long hours of work in cold places left them too tired to write letters home, and long distance phone calls were at their pre-cellular highs.

On weekends—or less frequently—these men, my father among them, came home and filled their time with the chores they once did in the evenings, after a day of work at the smelter—chopping and hauling wood, mending roofs, and tinkering with hot water heaters and furnaces and other appliances too expensive to replace. Such homework, combined with their migration to job sites, left them with little time for instruction.

Twenty-five years after the smelter in Anaconda closed, my son toddles toward me, a blue Lego block in each hand. They were connected when he took them out of his toybox. Now, he's pulled them apart and can't get them to go back together.

At fourteen months old, he just doesn't have that kind of manual dexterity. So he brings the blocks to me, sure that his father can help.

He holds the blocks out to me, but I don't take them, partially because my hands are blistered and sore from pounding nails all afternoon, mostly because it's the wrong thing to do. I take his tiny, delicately boned hands in mine, and I guide the blocks back together. They conjoin with an audible pop, and he grins widely—exposing a mouth already almost filled with teeth, straight and strong and white.

John ambles away from me at his fastest stagger, lurching and swaying but not falling down. He holds the Legos proudly above his head, entirely unaware of the price of copper.

I hated Nevada the whole time I lived there, and I'm pretty sure Nevada hated me back. But right at the end, just before we packed the house and drove away, Nevada gave me something worth having. Ironically enough, this Nevada-inspired moment produced an essay that was published in a Montana-based literary journal, Whitehorse Review.

Push
September 2011

WHEN MY SON turns his back, I plant myself and push with both hands. His yellow SpongeBob t-shirt is damp with sweat. This sends him flying, blonde hair flashing in sunlight so glaring it has weight. Coconut trails in John's wake, lingering remnant of the cheap sun block lathered on his pale shoulders.

The swing's chains squeal in rusty pain as he reaches the top of his arc and barrels back toward me, laughing. John's twin sister hangs from the monkey bars, fully extended and impossibly tall, to my eyes. I know that Samantha's hands are black from friction twists against tarnished pipes, and a vague smell of metal will follow her until bath time.

We visit the playground often since they graduated kindergarten. This is a place they know. The basketball hoops are low, which works for us. We are not tall people. A school-owned basketball, left out when the final recess bell rang in June, rests beneath the slide, and I know it will be hot to the touch even though it's in the shade. By the end of summer, if the basketball is still here, it will be bleached-white.

In a month, Elizabeth and I will take John and Sam on vacation, and they'll never see this home again. Everything will be packed, hauled, and unpacked in their absence, their bedrooms in Nevada remade in Montana, where work now takes me. There are heat shimmers baking upwards in this high desert that has been home for six years, but as a native of the Rocky Mountains, I do not fear Montana winters. I grew up in their violent rhythm of cold and heat, comfortably ear-popping through their radical changes in elevation.

In northern Nevada, my children have left their infancy and toddlerhood, and the seasons have made sense. Only the value of housing has been unpredictable.

After three hard pushes, John tells me to stop. I take the swing next to him, wedge myself into its curved rubber seat, and get a running start. I fit badly into this cradle designed for a child, and both hips begin to throb. I strain at the chains, leaning forward and backward in a stationary dance with momentum that I remember instinctively. My shoulders ache as I race, first unconsciously and then deliberately, to catch up with and pass my son.

A year of forced inactivity has left me both under-muscled and overweight.

At the top of each arc, the chains go slack. Just enough to make my stomach flutter. I have to fix my eyes on the roof of the school to keep from getting sick.

I pump so hard that one Birkenstock flies off, crossing a hopscotch grid and bouncing onto the court of a ball game I don't know. The grid lines are clear, but the game's name, painted upon the blacktop, has been scuffed away by small shoes. The sun pushes a hot tar tang out of this playground space, offering a patched pothole aroma that's out of place, given that nothing here is newer than the Carter presidency.

When my speed matches John's, we look at each other and smile, revealing the dimples we share. We fall into perfect synchronization for two full swings, eyes locked and hair flopping, mine starting to gray in irregular patterns. Thirty-four years separate us, and we pump our legs outwards on the upswing, inwards on the down.

John's eyes are enormous and brown, and he doesn't need glasses, as I did.

Samantha stands beside her mother, simultaneously clicking pictures and jumping up and down. Those shots will be both blurred and badly aimed, but I will keep them.

Rather than pull ahead, I reach out one-handed and grab John's nearest chain. I keep us swinging together. I force the rhythm to remain the same for both of us.

I am drunk with this moment of perfect fatherhood.

We begin to swing unevenly, staggering out of harmony.

"Dad!" John yells at me, his voice rising in exasperation. "Let go!"

I let go, but not right away.

Being a father, I find, is making it easier, bit by bit, to write about my sister. Stacie would have been a great aunt for John and Sam. I visit her regularly to talk about them, but they don't come along. I can't talk to the dead when I have an audience.

Similar Differences
March 2013

WHEN I WAS seven, my thirteen-year-old sister was killed in an accident near Georgetown Lake. As young as I was, I already understood the differences between us. Stacie loved to hunt, loved to fish, loved to water ski. She was good with her hands and took a natural interest in engines—and was an avid motorcycle rider and go-cart driver. She could effortlessly swing a bat and catch a ball. Stacie managed all of this with ease, and she got excellent grades in school during the whole time. I have family stories, photographs, report cards, and a trunk filled with trophies and ribbons to confirm all of this.

I didn't, wasn't, couldn't, wouldn't.

We were separated by our ages, but we were separated by a huge gulf of contrasting ability and interest. Worse, we were separated by a cultural chasm of understanding, one I bore the brunt of. Stacie, particularly because of her age, could walk and talk her way through the world as a tomboy. She was a girl, of course, but no one thought it odd that a Montana girl would hunt, ride bikes and snowmobiles, ski, etc. and so forth. She could get her hands greasy while still not confusing anyone about who she was.

I went the other way. I liked to read and wasn't any good—seriously, not any good—at catching a baseball. I was small, really small, and just didn't have any enthusiasm for physical activities like riding or skilled activities like building things from the ground up. I was afraid of the water—in my defense I saw *Jaws* at an extraordinarily young age—and refused to ski on it. I got upset easily and cried with little provocation. I did badly in school, once refusing to skip in PE for weeks—until my teacher told my mother. Then I learned just to spite her. I was afraid of confrontation and would back down, even when throwing a punch was a pretty good—and reasonably acceptable, age-appropriate—response to the situation.

Even writing that paragraph makes me feel like a sissy, a word I use with all of its devastating connotations. Montana boys were supposed to be...something...and I wasn't. My sister was a better Montana boy than I was, really.

Eventually, most of those things changed, I suppose. I learned to ski (downhill—I'm still a little freaked out by deep water) and did so for many years—and expect to begin again, now that my children are old enough to learn. I never became a sportsman, but I did become a knowledgeable fan and a father who never misses his kids' flag football games or wrestling matches. I learned to swing a hammer, turn a screwdriver, and sometimes simply dive into a mechanical project even if I didn't know how to get out the other side. I never learned to throw much of a punch, but I did learn that the best way to avoid most fights was to have absolutely no fears about being punched—a mindset that doesn't exactly lead to victory but keeps away the lingering shame of not being tough enough (whatever that means).

I came to terms with my past long ago, partially by writing about it, mostly just by growing up—growing up and realizing that manhood, like womanhood, is a culturally defined thing that changes over time. (Like many men damaged by growing to adulthood in the 1980s, I wear my hair long. When I hear some snide remark about this, I'm always a little surprised. First, I'm surprised because I thought prejudice against hippies pretty much died with the Nixon administration. Second, because if a hippie-hater would bother to glance at the change in his pocket—it's always a guy—he'd notice that those Founding Fathers weren't exactly sporting Marine haircuts.) With my twins, now seven years old, I see so much of my family's pattern repeating.

Samantha's tough and always has been. When something—anything—knocked her down, she bounced right back up again. If it was her brother who knocked her down, or some hapless kid at daycare, she came up swinging. She's endlessly engaged with physical activities—riding her bike, rollerskating, playing catch, kicking a football from one side of the yard to the other. This is where she finds happiness, and she's never, ever had a problem getting her hands dirty.

Samantha sometimes exhausts me—not because of a lack of love or enthusiasm but because I'm still me, even now that I'm a father. I still prefer less-than-physical activities, still prefer to read, still prefer watching a sport to playing it. I love my daughter and do everything I can to spend active time with her, but I know in my heart that she'd have fallen deeply in love with her aunt Stacie.

My son is me. John likes to read. He likes to play video games and would do so for hour after hour if I didn't monitor his screen time. He's not much of a bike rider and isn't into rollerskating. He likes learning to ski but wears his heart on his sleeve. (During a recent lesson, an instructor criticized him for not learning, yet, to stop quickly. As far as I can tell, the whole comment this teenage skier made to my son was, "Not cool." When John told me that, he burst into tears.)

I'm middle aged and mild-tempered (usually), and I can take a deep breath and then help my son get his emotions under control. But it's hard. Like me, John's a Montana boy. Even though I lived through the confusion he's going through now, even though we share similarities in so many ways, it's hard not to become upset by his tears, hard not to say some hurtful and inappropriate thing like "man up."

At nine, Sam knows all she needs to know about Aristotle's "division" topos and the either/or fallacy. Our lunchtime dialogue offers proof:

"Sam, do you want six chicken nuggets or eight?"

"Six. I would prefer four, but apparently that's not an option."

I worry a lot about the kind of dad I am. There are no perfect fathers, but there are degrees of good and bad, with a ton of variance in each gray area. As I age, little about me mellows, though. If anything, I think I'm winding up tighter and tighter as I get practice at fatherhood. And here I thought that drinking was the only thing you get worse at the longer you do it...

Becoming that Dad
December 2012

WHEN I WAS growing up in Anaconda, my father coached Little League. He took this job seriously. Very seriously. Too seriously, he admits now, nearly four decades later. His enthusiasm for the game led him to attempt to teach tactical game-play to kids who had, in many cases, never held a bat before. If the team won, he took everyone to the A&W on the edge of town, the entire cadre crammed into the back the brown International Harvester we normally used to haul wood.

There weren't many trips to A&W.

But there were tantrums. When calls were bad and catches were fumbled, he cursed, stomped, threw anything close to hand—a bat, a helmet, some unlucky kid's soda. He wasn't alone. Many parents, especially the fathers, yelled. They yelled at their sons when they did well, screaming instructions about how the boys could have done better. They yelled when their sons struck out, both at the boys who swung and the umpires who made calls.

There were a lot of tears shed in the dust-smelling dugouts. I was the batboy, and even I was regularly yelled at.

I didn't see anything wrong with this at the time, and neither did anyone else. Yelling and crying were just a part of playing sports.

I live in Dillon now and am the father of seven-year-old twins, John and Samantha. For six years, I raised them beneath the rhetoric of "do your best" and "it's all about how you play the game." Then they got involved in flag football and Little Guy Wrestling...and I became That Dad.

It started when the Broncos played the Vikings. Samantha, playing quarterback for the Broncos, ran the ball toward the endzone—a pack of milling, mostly confused 1st graders around her. She leaped over a Viking—who, to be honest, tripped and fell down right in front of her, an accident rather than an attempt to make a play. She cut to the sideline, only feet away from where I stood cheering.

And then a Viking player tackled her. They hit the ground in a heap, my daughter buried beneath a boy maybe fifteen pounds heavier. Her glasses flew off. The ball flew out of bounds.

I freaked out.

One minute I was standing along the sidelines, cheering with all the other parents. The next minute I was having an out-of-body experience, bellowing at the coach to get that boy out of the game and at the referee to do something about this massive, unacceptable breaking of the "just pull the flag" rule that's at the heart of *flag* football.

Sam got up, got back into the huddle, and ran for a touchdown on the next play. She scored again a few plays later.

I seethed. I stared at the boy who'd brought my daughter down. I searched the other sideline for the parents who were responsible for raising such a monster. I glared at the Vikings' coach. I behaved exactly like all the parents from my Little League memories, and I knew I was doing it. But it was impossible for me to stop.

When football ended and Little Guy Wrestling began, I swore I wouldn't be That Dad again, wouldn't fly off the handle and yell at anyone—not a coach, not a participant, not a parent. I kept this promise through Saturday after Saturday of sitting in crowded, hot gyms filled with young wrestlers and their families. I recorded each match with my video camera and never said a word—leaving my wife and others to cheer. No matter how many parents around me howled at their children and at the referees and judges, I remained silent. Until John made it to State, wrestling at Pee-Wee 46 weight class.

Samantha made State in her weight class, too, but came down with the flu literally the night before the tournament. She stayed home with my wife, while my father and I took John to Helena, where he would ultimately win every match and take first in his ranking.

But as he won match after match, sometimes by scoring more points, sometimes by pinning boys much stronger than him, he cried. Tears ran down his small face almost from the minute each match began until it was over. He cried when he was ahead on points. He cried when he was behind. He cried when he got pinned. He cried after he pinned someone else. John wasn't the only boy crying—there were tears everywhere.

I could feel my patience unstitch with each tear. On an intellectual level, I knew that he was crying because of the pressure. He was at State. He was only seven—and just barely seven, at that. He was sur-rounded by hundreds of screaming, cheering families. His mother wasn't there. His sister wasn't there. His grandfather watched from the stands, so all he had near at hand was me. I understood all of this.

But John's tears quite literally infuriated me, and my fury shamed me. I hugged him. I encouraged him. I walked with him to and from the locker room. We shared slices of pizza and took turns playing his Nintendo, where I pretended that I was letting him win (when, in truth, I was having my virtual clock cleaned).

I did what I could to get him through the day, and by the time we stopped in Butte for dinner, he was strutting. He marched to the counter at Burger King, ordered his chicken meal, and announced loudly to the clerk that he was State Champ in wrestling. He was fine.

I was the one who was upset, and my father knew it. As we drove the last sixty miles to Dillon, he did perhaps the only thing he could to talk me down: He told me about coaching Little League, about the tears that he and other parents caused young players to shed, about his own shame at being That Dad.

Flag football starts soon. Little Guy Wrestling isn't much after that. Whenever something stressful occurs, I tell myself that I'm going to take deep breaths and think about Little League.

*I began watching horror movies when I was young. Really
young.* Jaws *is one of the first films I remember seeing. Same
with* The Amityville Horror, *although in that case, I also
remember reading the book and listening to it (on one vinyl
33rpm album after another) with my great grandmother.
Audio books didn't exist then as a consumer product, but
the legally blind (like my great grandmother) could join a
club that sent out books on 8-track and vinyl and cassettes,
later on. Nothing much was denied me when it came to
entertainment. Across my entire childhood, I remember only
once being taken out of the theatre for a few minutes. That
happened during one of the sex scenes in the film* Excalibur.
*Raising my own kids, then, I haven't always drawn a clear
line between what is and what isn't age appropriate.*

Games, Movies, and Childhood Magic
May 2013

I'M THE FATHER who goes quiet when a conversation turns toward
the things everyone else denies their children. My best friend's daughter didn't see an R-rated movie until she was thirteen. My neighbor's
kids are allowed to play only Lego games on their Wii. My nephew is
allowed to watch only Nickelodeon when he visits his grandparents,
and his family doesn't own a television at all. If parental censorship
is a continuum, then I'm at the other end from these responsible
decision makers.

My twins are eight years old. For years, I have denied them almost
nothing.

At three, my son's favorite movie was *300*, and he would, daily,
lead his toddler army at daycare. Lincoln Log sword held high, he
would rouse his troops: "This is where we hold them! This is where
we fight! This is where they die! Spartans, prepare for glory!" He

had it all memorized. I have video. My daughter—less interested in films—would sit on my lap as I played World of Warcraft. She watched my troll hunter fight giant spiders and lose. Multiple times. She mocked me.

We watched *Jurassic Park* together, and the velociraptors-stalking-children scenes didn't trouble them. We watched all of the Harry Potter films, and even the Dementors didn't upset them. No crawling into my lap. No nightmares. Even Shelob didn't creep them out...and I'm still a little bothered by that particular massive arachnid even at the age of 42.

"It's just pretend," my daughter once told me.

Growing up, I wasn't censored at all, and I spent most Saturday afternoons, once cartoons were over, watching double features of black-and-white horror from another era—*Creature from the Black Lagoon, Them!*, and endless variations and combinations of *Dracula, Frankenstein*, and *The Wolfman*. My wife was not raised on a steady diet of horror, and we've agreed not to expose the kids to this particular genre of film or gaming. Yet. We've done alright with keeping them away from the horror films, but survival horror gaming is ubiquitous. Even though they don't play Dead Island at home, they play it with their friends during recess. Same with the Halo franchise, Call of Duty, and Resident Evil. The school, which has a policy against students bringing any type of toy weapon onto campus, can't bar imagined video game content from its play yard. And we have a simple arrangement: They're allowed to hear a video game character say anything, no matter how profane, as long as I don't hear them repeat it.

So I go quiet when other parents discuss their censorship efforts, and I only passively enforce a largely pointless ban on horror movies and games. I suspect other parents judge and find me wanting.

I'm ok with that. And I'm really ok with the fact that technology has allowed me to share my own childhood with my children.

I grew up in the age of the Atari. The 2600 disappeared decades ago but was resurrected as a stand-alone plug-and-play console preloaded with several dozen games. Most of them are awful, and John and Samantha don't mind telling me so. But Pitfall has withstood the test of time. We bond in the present over a piece of my past.

As a child, my year was built around specific television events: Charlie Brown marked every Halloween and Thanksgiving, as the Grinch marked Christmas. There were dozens of others, from *Mad Monster Party* to *Little Drummer Boy*. But these seasonal offerings were only the regularly scheduled part of the program. My year was also built around annual showings of *The Wizard of Oz*, *The Ten Commandments*, *The Hobbit*. These programs continue to be a part of my life, although I'm able to share them with my children mostly because of Netflix.

Technology helps with the magic, too.

My twins learned of Santa Claus from childhood's films. They never had to ask how Santa could get down a chimney. Tim Allen showed them.

As they're getting older, the dreams of early childhood are ending. Recently we watched *Rise of the Guardians*, a cartoon featuring everyone from a mime-like Sandman to an Aussie Easter Bunny. They loved the movie. So did I.

The next day, they sat beside me at church during the funeral of my great uncle. During the service, my son leaned in and told me, out of the blue, "Dad, I don't think I really believe in Santa or the Tooth Fairy or any of that anymore." I suspect his belief has only lasted this long because of film, but the situation was an odd one, and I whispered back to him the only thing that came to mind: "Son, all that really matters is that we believe in love. That's the real magic."

An early story by Samantha Borrowman, 1ˢᵗ grade.

✓ My own idea goblins

Now, write about your main idea here. Write at least 3 sentences.

Goblin are not reel they are mack bleeve. Gobins are cool and creepy and spooky. and Gobins are green and red. and Gobins feel ruber.

Wow! Way to stick to your main topic ✓

I attract weirdness. It's a trait I share with my mother. If I'm in a crowd of 100 people and a guy walks in wearing a Superman costume and a pair of bunny ears, he'll talk to me. Normally, this isn't really an issue, though. It leads to interesting conversations. I sat at the airport bar in Reno, Nevada, and ate terrible chicken wings while the woman next to me ate the same terrible wings and told me about how she'd come to town only to apply for work at one of the local brothels. You can't buy conversation like that. No pun intended. Puns are the lowest form of humor. But sometimes this magnetic pull brings in an individual who isn't bolted together quite right. I describe one of them here (and hope, with no real hope, that he'll be the last).

At the Corner of Cornell and Crazy
January 2013

IF I CLIMB my family tree, it doesn't take long to reach some rotten branches, generations where prison records were as common as high school graduation certificates. My great-grandfather's criminal history spanned three decades, beginning with "theft of a horse," moving through forgery, and culminating in rape. One great-uncle went AWOL from the Army, beat a man, and stole his car. Another great-uncle, a corrupt police officer, may have been murdered—not because of the beer and money he stole but because he stopped and planned to testify against those who didn't.

I bring this up not for the sake of revelation but for explanation. There's a reckless streak in me that's probably genetic, an impulse to walk toward trouble rather than to back away from it. When my children are older, it'll make me a bad role model if I don't have it under control. They're seven. I have a little more time.

They are the same age as many of the victims of the shooting in Connecticut on Friday, December 14, 2012. I can't stop thinking about that, especially because of the run-in I had with a local bully that same morning.

Cornell's one of the many streets that hits campus like an arrow, crossing town and ending at Atlantic, where students with early classes take up the parking before I can even get my kids out the door and to the bus stop. So by the time I come to work—where parking isn't free and is out of my price range—I have to park on a side street. I'm conscientious about not blocking driveways, about being close to the curb, and about not parking in a yellow zone. I never gave this situation a thought.

But someone was thinking about parking and about me, and he was getting mad.

When I pulled into an empty spot on that Friday morning, CrazyGuy was waiting for me. He's maybe seventy, seems like a cross between John McCain and Grandpa Simpson, and we've met before.

A year ago, I crossed Atlantic street, and he stomped up to me to ask, "You like stopping traffic?" I was so baffled that I had to ask him twice to explain what he was talking about. He was angry that I'd crossed Atlantic, going from campus into his neighborhood, and had caused traffic to back up three or four car lengths. I told him twice that I'd crossed legally, but he shrugged that off. Worse, and weirder, was the fact that he kept reaching out and touching my shoulder—until I finally told him, "Stop touching me. Now."

The encounter was odd because he both touched me and asked where I was going. I told the story to friends, laughed, and generally forgot it. Until December 14, 2012.

When I parked that morning, CrazyGuy was waiting for me. "Why don't you park on campus?" he asked. I told him there was no parking and that this was a public street. This set him off, and he began to rant about how he paid taxes, about how the street was his, about how if I had any decency I wouldn't park by his house.

If I was any farther from his house, then I'd have been on another block entirely. Then he took three steps toward me.

A smart man would have backed off. But I am a product of my genetics, and I took two steps at him, explaining in a less than calm manner that I owned a home, paid taxes, and didn't care what he thought. He got closer and accused me of parking in front of his neighbor's driveway the day before. I denied it, but I also had a sudden moment of clarity.

CrazyGuy wasn't just mad at me today. He was mad at me yesterday, too. Today, he was waiting for me. I pulled out my phone, dialed 911, and told the dispatcher to send an officer immediately: "There's about to be a fight."

CrazyGuy scampered away, since he's apparently no more than a grown-up bully, and I'd called him on his nonsense, but I thought a lot about him, and about our confrontation, as I watched the news that day. Before I called the police, we'd almost come to blows over nothing, over the fact that I was legally parked nowhere near his house, and he didn't like it.

But what if he'd had a gun? What if I'd had one?

This led me to a father's question that I can't stop considering: How often in our daily lives do we come into contact with someone who is, like CrazyGuy, legitimately off in some way? When we do, we minimize their danger, as I did when this guy got angry because I crossed the street in a crosswalk.

We assume that dangerous levels of insanity only occur rarely, but we're wrong. Odd behavior happens again and again with someone like CrazyGuy, and it only escalates.

I still park near the corner of Cornell and Crazy. I have to. And I don't know how our next confrontation will end, but I do know I'll see him again.

I can't stop thinking about my second-grade twins, about men like CrazyGuy, about the fact that irrational behavior only expands and never contracts. When a tragedy like that of December 14, 2012, occurs, we reel back in horror and wonder why no one saw the violence coming.

But my bet is that someone did. Maybe someone who did nothing more than cross the street or park.

If CrazyGuy was a one-time sort of encounter, I might not mind. But encountering the odd is something I seem to do every few years—encountering someone truly warped to the danger point. I've written about two of them in the past, even, in fragmentary bits under the working title "Schizos."

I write a lot about family. Obviously. It baffles me when others are reluctant to talk about the alcoholics, manic depressives, and criminals that showed up to every family reunion. In my mind, that's where some of the top-shelf stories are to be found. But there are plenty of other stories worth telling. My 4xs-great grandfather on my mother's side, for example, rode with the 7th Cavalry...from which he deserted. In the early 1920s, he applied for a disability pension, claiming he'd been shot through the right hand in Dakota Territory while still in the service of the US Army. His request was denied, and he was told that although Congress had agreed not to prosecute deserters from the Indian Wars, he was still, legally, a deserter. As a deserter, he naturally had no right to a disability pension. I haven't told his story yet, and parts of it I still can't fill in for myself. But there are stories there, and I'll get to them. None of it, I try to explain to my children, is secret, and it's too good to keep private. He's not the only deserter in the family, after all.

Private? Or Secret?
August 2013

IN THE SUMMER of 1989, I worked at Canyon Lodge in Yellowstone Park. Mostly, I was charged with the awesome responsibility of keeping the salad bar stocked. About six months ago I told my son, John, about this as we worked on his wooden derby car for Cub Scouts. In particular, I told him about how kitchen safety required that anyone coming around a blind corner while carrying a hot pan must call out loudly: "Hot pan coming around!" John watches cooking shows with me sometimes, so this makes sense to him. As I told him more about the people I worked with, I found myself talking about Lowell, a young guy from Wyoming who yelled something every time he went around a kitchen corner, no matter what he was carrying: "Hot pan coming around! Well, not so hot that it's gonna burn you, but it's still pretty hot."

John found this hilarious. Now he repeats the line whenever we're in the kitchen. Then he laughs. Samantha, his twin sister, laughs too. She didn't hear the story from me, but John told it to her.

That story from the summer of '89 doesn't really matter. It's only important because my son, and now my daughter, remember it. They might always remember it. It might be something they share with their own children some day.

Some stories do matter, though; the stories that define the family's values, that explain how and where my wife and I met, that explain who we all are and how we got this way.

I tell my kids about two of my great uncles, June and Jack, both paratroopers at Normandy and both at the siege of Bastogne. I tell them about the summer my father worked at a bowling alley, sanding lanes and making better money than when he stocked grocery shelves. I tell them about my great-grandmother, describing the hours I spent sitting in her kitchen as she cooked chicken noodle soup or baked angel food cake. I tell them about my sister, long gone, and the days we spent riding her yellow motorcycle.

They hear it all and sometimes ask questions. Mostly, they just go along with what I'm doing, understanding that I'm mostly talking about people they'll never meet and places they'll never go—places that might not even exist any more. Some of this will be remembered (just as I remember some of what I was told) but most will be forgotten.

I tell them the good things I know, the things that might interest and engage them. I tell them age-appropriate versions of the stories about their 4th-time great grandfather, an original pioneer to Utah, a one-time Texas Ranger, a veteran of both the Mexican and the Utah War, a defense attorney for Brigham Young, personal friend to Sam Houston. Good stuff. They like hearing about him.

They don't yet know that he was a polygamist who had six wives and twenty-seven children. They know about the wives and the kids, but polygamy is complicated for an 8-year-old. I'll tell them when they are older, but for now it's something I'll keep openly private.

Not secret. Just private. There's a difference, and it's one I want them to understand early.

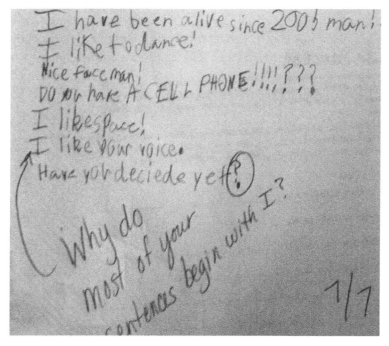

I have been alive since 2005 man!
I like to dance!
Nice face man!
Do you have A CELL PHONE!!!!???
I likespace!
I like your voice.
Have you deciede yet?
Why do most of your contences begin with I?
7/7

Sam...receiving odd criticism about her choice of pronoun.

They know some of their more distant relatives have done prison time, but they don't yet know half the story. They know that twins run in the family. They don't know that jailbreaks run in the family, (two in Idaho and one in Montana), just like alcoholism and suicide. They don't know they're related to two Army deserters—one in the 1950s and one in the late 1800s. Or to a dirty policeman in a small Montana town, who was possibly murdered to keep him from testifying against his fellow officers. They don't know about the horse thieves, forgers, rapists and strong-arm robbers. Plus, well, a slew of petty thieves.

John and Sam know a bit of this, just a reference here and there. Most importantly, they know that none of this is secret. Secrets are heavy, hard to carry and laborious to maintain. Secrets aren't worth their weight in whispers.

But explaining the fine distinctions between something that's private and something that's secret is too much—too much for me to manage, too much for them to process. So I tell stories, stories about the private life of the family, all of it public record in one way or another, none of it secret.

Hot pan coming around.

I love my boots. I keep them in my office, wearing walking shoes as I go to and fro. But the boots go with everything... everything that I wear, anyway. I started my career wearing full suits, even ties, every day. Then I stopped wearing ties. Then the slacks got replaced by jeans. Now I keep a suit coat hanging on my office chair and tend to wear fleece vests...that I originally bought at a grocery store. The clothes reflect my comfort with my life, I suppose, especially the slouch boots.

My Son's First Pair of Cowboy Boots
November 2013

MY SON, JOHN, got his first pair of cowboy boots a few weeks back—brown, embroidered on the top (starting at the toe box) and sides, a zipper running partially up the outside of each shaft. Stylin'. I had some when I was younger than him—he's eight now—but once those wore out, I didn't have another pair again until I was almost thirty. He loves these boots, and he wears them nearly every day.

After a couple weeks of playground use, though, those brown boots were looking a little shabby. So, one morning before school, I dug out my shine kit—a long buffing brush with dark bristles, a can of "neutral" Kiwi Polish (apparently I'm out of both brown and black), and a few old cotton socks. I keep all of this in an original GI Joe box, which is long—since it held a 12" action figure—and has a lid that slides on and off. If the thing wasn't stained inside with polish, then it might be worth something all on its own.

I sat on the living room floor. My son took his boots off and handed them to me. I put one sock over my right hand, fingers shoved all the way to the toe, and pulled up a glob of polish—which I then smeared all over the right boot.

John didn't want to say anything, but I could tell that he was dubious about how this process was going to turn out. He's seen me in action before, and he's seen my plans go astray regardless of my level of confidence. Just ask him about last year's Derby Car for Scouts. Working through that project involved a lot more use of power tools than it should have, plus multiple messy coats of paint in too small of a room for such work to be truly safe.

As I wiped polish all over the boot, really rubbing it into each nook and seam, I explained what I was doing, explained that shining boots was, at its heart, a pretty simple process (assuming we're talking about dirty boots that are just dusty, rather than about boots that are caked with mud or manure). Wipe off dust. Wipe on polish. Buff. Wipe down a bit more. Do the other boot.

Somewhere in there, as I finished coating the first boot with that clear polish and then began buffing, I trailed off. John was still watching, still paying attention to how boots should be shined, but I was lost in the process, lost in the past.

The smell of the polish is rich and warm. Putting it on each boot is a greasy process that doesn't leave my fingers greasy...but somehow manages to leave the suggestion that they're greasy. The sound of the brush—a sort of whish, whish—is soft and low. As I buffed that polish into each boot, bringing the cheap leather to a dark and golden shine, I was flooded with memories of my father.

Dad wore cowboy boots all the time when I was a kid. He kept the boxes that they came in when he bought them, so he always had a safe storage place, and his shine rags and polish went into an old blue shoebox, one that he still has. He used the same buffing brush I have now, a gift he passed along on some random weekend two decades ago, during a discussion of the quality of the work shoes I was buying at Payless.

It occurs to me not that he was probably trying to point out politely that my shoes were cheap because they looked cheap...but a great shine would help.

Dad shined his cowboy boots all the time, my memory tells me, at least every weekend (usually more than one pair, since he had several at any given time). For five years, he was a deputy Sheriff in Deer Lodge County, and he regularly shined the boots that went with that uniform, too. When the Anaconda Company collapsed and economics forced him to take work at the Hanford Nuclear Site, on the security team, those combat boots needed almost daily shining.

The same rags, the same brush, the same brand of Kiwi Polish.

The same rich smells and smooth, repetitive sounds over and over again, from the time of my earliest memories in Anaconda to the time of my most recent visit to Washington.

I could not polish my son's boots before school that morning without thinking about my father. He never exactly told me "Do this, then this, then this." He just showed me, again and again, what should be done—both in terms of what it literally took to make boots clean and shiny and in terms of what it took to look professional, to look my best (even if finances did keep me in a cheap loafer until I could finally afford boots). It was a lesson that took hold, apparently, at a level I never expected. Never even guessed at until I lived it.

When John got home that night, his boots were scuffed and dirty again—apparently because he drags his feet when he's manually slowing down his swing. The toes were rubbed right down to the point where the surface-level color was completely gone. I couldn't have been happier. I pulled out the GI Joe box and set out my socks, my brush, my polish. I lay these things in a loose arc on the floor in front of me, John's boots close to hand.

As he watched, I shined them again, shined them for him for the second time. There's not a doubt in my mind that he could do this himself, now, if I'd let him. But it's hard to give up. When I shine John's boots, I'm granted one of those moments of time travel that only parents truly understand—one of those moments where the past and the present fold over on one another so fully that it happens with an almost audible click. Even better, I see the past and the present as they move into the future.

John and I will shine our boots together soon. Eventually, I'll give him the big brush that I use, probably when he's been in college for a couple years. He'll need it, since that will be the one he's used to working on his own leather. And I can buy another...knowing that some day he'll teach his own son to shine boots.

I worry about money constantly...until Christmas comes. Then I pull out all the stops while simultaneously telling everyone not to make a fuss over me. Last Christmas, I did all of the wrapping, and the results were...mixed.

My Wrapping Privileges May Be Revoked
December 2013

CHRISTMAS BRINGS OUT the sadist in me. It's a flaw I've always been aware of but have always managed to hold in check. I don't think my family knows. They will.

This year my wife left me in charge of wrapping all of the packages that aren't for me. Normally this doesn't happen, most likely because I wrap things really, really badly. I go through rolls of paper. Rolls. Everything gets too many layers, too much tape. My package corners tend not to be well creased. By the time I'm done, every gift usually looks like some sort of freakish but well-intentioned Improvised Christmas Device.

It isn't pretty.

But that's not sadism. Here's the sadism: I use boxes for almost everything. Even things that already come in boxes. I put boxes in bigger boxes and wrap both of them, one inside the other. I don't do this because unwrapping presents is fun, but because it is slow. Maddeningly slow. A child's equivalent of long security lines at the airport.

Merry Christmas morning to my eight-year-old twins. Expect delays. That should not make me smile. It does. I accept this.

So that's a little sadistic, but I get worse: I put a handful of gravel in the box, producing a very satisfying sound of broken glass (and probably a little anxiety) when shaking is done. Or I toss a few pens and pencils in, plus a few seashells. The sound that box makes when shaken is just, well, odd. It certainly doesn't sound like an XboxOne game, to me or to anyone. Another package gets The Silent Treatment, where I use a large, weighty quilt and pillow not only to make the box freakishly heavy for its size but also to keep the actual gift from making a sound. It's a big, heavy box of mystery.

All of this may mean that my wrapping privileges are revoked in 2014. I won't argue if that happens. The punishment would be fitting. Christmas wrapping-related sadism aside, I'd like to think I'm a pretty good guy, a pretty good parent who cares about kids—mine and those around me.

It hurts me desperately, then, when I'm suddenly confronted by one of those moments when I realize that not only is a child's life harder than I ever dreamed, but there's nothing I can do about it unless things actually get worse. And even then there's not much to do to help.

This sort of helpless revelation happened recently when a friend came over to play with my twins, something he's done—coming over to the house and staying anywhere from one to four hours—for years. His mother dropped him off, which was slightly unusual (since normally he just rides his bike), and all of them began to play Uno. I couldn't see the game from my chair in the living room, but I could chart its progress by the sounds. There's a special scream of delighted frustration that's unique to someone who has just been dealt a Draw Four by a friend.

After only a short time, though, maybe as little as thirty minutes, our visitor's father came to the door. He wasn't there to get his son, though. He stood in my doorway, even though I invited him in, and called his boy outside. They spoke at length, although I don't know what was said. I learned early on never to read over someone's shoulder and never to eavesdrop. I won't do either.

When my kids' friend came back in to rejoin the Uno game, the boy's father called to me. "His mother and I had a fight," he opened—already telling me more about his/their life than I wanted to know, I guess. "She left for Bozeman and dropped him off here. If she comes to get him, don't let her take him. Call me."

My immediate response was probably to blink and look stupid.

"Well," I said to this father worried about his upset wife taking physical custody of their son, "my wife's running some errands soon, and she was planning on dropping him off at your place on the way." That was actually true, which is the only reason I had anything to say at all. Otherwise, I'm sure I would have just nodded pointlessly.

"Perfect," he told me. "That'll work just perfect."

He left, and I went back to my chair. Within the hour, my wife dropped the boy off at home, after making sure he had our phone number and knew that he could call if he ever, ever needed us—or he could just come by.

But the odd hypocrisy wasn't lost on me: "Here's my number, kiddo. Call me if you need me, and let's just ignore the fact that I think you probably need me right now. Don't forget your hat."

I haven't been able to stop thinking about it, haven't been able to stop mulling over the "What can I do?" and "What should I have done?"

The second one is easy—if ugly—to answer. I did exactly what I had to do. Legally, there's no way I could tell the mother, "No, you aren't taking your son home. Just wait outside while I call his father, your husband."

This event happened on my 43rd birthday. If I'd had that conversation with the mother, I would have spent the night of my birthday in jail for kidnapping.

And I wouldn't have had a defense to make, which brings me to the "What can I do?" in my thinking. To my knowledge, the boy isn't being abused in any way. Not at all. There's never been a mark on him, and I've never heard him say anything that suggests there's just a mark I'm not seeing. I've never even heard one of his parents raise a voice in anger to him.

Parental arguing is not abusing this kid in a way that calls for my involvement. For any involvement, as far as I can tell.

In my careful, analytical, educated opinion, that sucks. But it doesn't suck in a way that screams "This is abuse!" The kid's parents just don't get along, apparently, and he's stuck in the middle. That's a sad story that's common.

But I can't stop thinking about it.

I can't stop thinking about him.

And it makes me sad.

It's December, and I've been sadistic in my present wrapping practices. I've been busy helping my son build a Secret Santa present for someone in his Scout troop. I've been figuring out how to contribute to KIND, a charitable organization that provides desks to schools in Africa.

Charity begins at home, the cliché says, and that's true. I can't do anything to help a boy, apparently, who is in a situation that's hard but not criminal. All I seem able to do is to support him, talk to him, encourage his continuing friendship with my twins.

It doesn't feel like much, not at any time of the year.

I'm surprised sometimes by how few pictures I actually take of my children. Last year, they played flag football, snowboarded, joined the swim team at the Y, and played soccer. They both played in a school "recorder" recital, and John was in the talent show—offering up his spin on a story he heard about a father taking his children to the zoo. I loved hearing my son, in his assumed role, talking about his children. Funny. He delivered it well, too, even acting the part of a smug ostrich. I have maybe twenty pictures, total, of all of this. Not one of them has been printed. Most are still just on my phone, not even posted to Facebook. Weird. I took more pictures of the kids when they were doing less.

Documentary Evidence
January 2014

MY TWINS ARE eight, and they love to watch "old" videos of themselves, especially those videos taken when they were two or three years old. We have a lot of these. Boxes full. Maybe six months before they were born, I bought a video camera, one of those that records directly onto a mini-DVD.

I filmed enough random life—my pregnant wife sitting in a rocking chair, the dog playing with a soccer ball—that I knew how to work most of the buttons and had a general sense of how long the batteries lasted. Then I never touched it again until the night the kids were born—filming their tiny bodies as they lay in the neo-natal intensive care (a mandatory precaution, given that they were premature). Their health was never really a problem, and they improved daily for the month of their stay in the NICU.

I don't think I ever put the camera down, not while they were in the hospital, not when they came home, not for the next four years or so. I filmed everything. I filmed them eating and playing, slapping each other and snuggling with each other, fighting over possession of a white and red rocking horse and sharing a bottle of milk as they sat hidden in a bottom cupboard. (That particular hiding spot never worked well: They threw plastic containers everywhere in order to make room for themselves, giggled constantly when they thought someone was looking for them, and always opened the door a crack to peek out. I pretended, consistently, to be the worst, most oblivious "It" to ever play hide and seek, however, so it all worked out.)

So the kids love to watch these mini-DVDs, and I'm happy to watch them, too. They don't make me cry or make me nostalgic, but they do remind me just how bad my memory is. A lot of their early life seems like it happened when I wasn't paying attention, even though I'm there in virtually every frame. I was writing a lot, teaching a lot, and speaking at a lot of conferences. I was always there, basically, but I just, well, wasn't always present.

I remember how much my daughter, still an infant, loved it when I'd lie on my back, lift her straight up, and blow on her belly through her t-shirt. She'd thrash, giggle, and squirm back into position so I could tickle her again. I remember that so well I can still feel her weight in my left forearm, feel the cotton shirt under my hand, smell the baby powder.

I don't think I would remember this if I didn't see it on the DVDs over and over again.

Same thing with my son's ritual greeting whenever I would come home from teaching a night class: We would stand at opposite sides of the coffee table (me on my knees, him atop his quivering legs). He'd let out a bellowing sort of grunt. I'd return the sound with a slightly different inflection. He'd grunt or holler or whatever, maybe slapping the table for emphasis. I'd do almost the same back to him. We'd verbally volley until he dissolved into laughter. I'd forgotten this ever happened. Ever. Until we watched the disc not long after Christmas.

John and Sam have a childhood, especially an early childhood, that's well documented. Aside from the video, there are pictures, of course. Endless pictures. Literally thousands of digital pictures. Only a few hundred (maybe) have been printed, though, which sometimes worries me. Nothing's worse for the storage of information than a shift in technology, and if the PC someday stops recognizing .jpg files, I'm in real trouble. And the secondary evidence is staggering—the school records, medical records, certificates of achievement, etc., etc., and so forth. It makes me realize how little of my own past exists.

Until I had twins, the only video of me that existed, as far as I know, would be random party footage from college—the sort of "Chug! Chug! Chug!" footage that isn't even worth raising an eyebrow over, now that every phone can instantly post HD video to Facebook. I have a range of pictures of myself, but there aren't that many from when I was very young. Some. Just not many.

And when it comes to infant pictures, I'd be shocked if I have more than a dozen different images (most of them with me in the background, rather than pictures "of" me). It has nothing to do with my family dynamic. Pictures just weren't taken as much when a roll of film (maybe big enough to hold two dozen separate images) had to be loaded, flash cubes had to be carried and attached to the camera, and then the film had to be taken to a place like Osco Drug to be developed (for several dollars per roll, if I'm remembering my 1970s and 1980s pricing). It was enough of a bother that one picture was enough: Pose the family. Snap. On to something else.

Now I take ten or fifteen shots every time the kids put on a costume, get on a stage, or hold a microphone. Why not? There's almost no effort involved, other than charging my phone and infrequently emptying my memory card. Of course, I rarely remember to do either. "Almost no effort" is, after all, not the same as "no effort."

Go back a generation, and there are even fewer pictures of my parents. I have less than a shoebox full, I'd guess, if I dumped them all together (and didn't include the hundreds I could print of them holding my kids…). There are occasional pictures of my grandparents and great grandparents, but it's generally a sort of Kodak desert when I look for them in my albums—and worse when I look beyond them.

Ironically—or maybe predictably—these are the relatives I tell John and Sam about the most. John Borrowman, Pearl Harbor survivor who sent his full pay home to his parents throughout the entire war (and then did the same for his wife when he was called back to fight in Korea). Why not? He could support himself perfectly well with his poker winnings. Jay and Jack, veterans of the airborne invasion of Normandy. June, who always told me about the turtle he owned in the 1920s (that he had to rescue from the neighbors on more than one occasion, neighbors always bent on opening that pet with a rock). Bob, who taught me to make mud pies and rock soup. Alice, who helped me scare a cousin so bad it took him years to truly forgive me, and he's never forgotten. Nick, Alice's husband, who would ask me obvious questions about American history and then rave about my intelligence.

The list goes on, forever, almost, to include cousins and old neighbors and a host of friends and acquaintances and people I shouldn't remember but do. Occasionally, I'll have a picture to support the narrative. Usually, there's nothing but the narrative arc itself—heavy on setting and character development, sometimes light on plot. When things really turned interesting, I'll have a newspaper story or prison record to help tell the tale. Most of those stories—those of crime and punishment—aren't quite eight-year-old appropriate.

I do what I can to remember all of it, all of them, and I share it with my twins. There's no record, sometimes, beyond my own faded and faulty recollections. But I do what I can. It's important.

Early in 2014, I was asked to give the keynote address at a conference in Atlanta, Georgia. While I was speaking to a full house, a man walked into the room and stopped maybe halfway up the central aisle. He just stood there. After maybe thirty seconds, I asked him, in my least reasonable voice, "Can I help you with something?" (Keep in mind that I'm the guy who was delivering a speech, so this question brought the proceedings to a screeching halt.) My diplomatic skills are stunted at best. Apparently the room had been double-booked; two of the graduate students who were handling the event's logistics (and keeping me from getting lost) bum rushed the guy out of the room, and I finished my speech. Some of that keynote address became the core of "Memories, Nightmares, and Sin."

Memories, Nightmares, and Sin
February 2014

All profound changes in consciousness, by their very nature, bring with them characteristic amnesias. Out of such oblivions, in specific historical circumstances, spring narratives.
—Benedict Anderson, *Imagined Communities*

MAYBE TWENTY YEARS ago, I was teaching nonfiction and writing about my childhood. In particular, I found myself writing about dreams—about nightmares so terrifying that their fragments remain with me even now, at 43. Like most of my early memories, I don't really have a timeline that I associate with these dreams—no context, no idea how old I might have been at the time they plagued me.

So I called my mother, which is a good strategy for pretty much every situation. I don't remember the exact dialogue. But I remember the question I asked: "How old was I when I had all those nightmares about being kidnapped?"

I remember waking up screaming night after night, remember my parents running into my room to comfort me. The memories are in fragments, but they have the color and texture of any other childhood memory. I remember the light from the small aquarium on my dresser shimmering, its shadows darting, until mom or dad would snap on the overhead light, its fluorescent glow eliminating all darkness.

So I asked my question about when this period of night terrors happened, and silence fell on the telephone line.

"That never happened," my mother finally said. She said it much nicer than it sounds, but her denial of a truth I remembered was complete.

Only a few weeks ago, I found myself in another role in a similar sort of conversation. I was in my living room, in my favorite brown chair, talking with my daughter. She's eight—the age I would guess I was, more or less, when I (maybe) had all those nightmares that I remember. Those nightmares my mother denies.

Somehow, Sam and I ended up talking about the weather, which hadn't yet turned polar, and then an odd thing happened. Samantha began by asking, "Dad, do you remember that one day last winter, when the weather was perfect?" She went on to describe the sparse cloud cover, which gave us almost full sun. She described how there was almost no snow on the ground, just a few dirty piles in the shade. She described how there was only a little wind.

Sam really got into this. I was tickled, since the writer in me loves to hear that much detail, while the parent in me just loves to see Sam get excited as she tells a story.

But her story was all setting and no action, so I finally asked her, "What were we doing?" She didn't even hesitate before giving me the answer: "We were playing catch with the football. The big one."

That's what she calls the regulation-size ball we have. It's nearly too big for her hands, but it's the only one I can catch. I seem to be Nerf-challenged. I found myself thinking about this conversation later. I haven't really stopped. I don't know if Sam was describing an actual, specific day, a day on the calendar that could have been recorded in factual terms. It's possible.

But she's wrong about the key event: Sam and I couldn't have been playing catch at any point last winter, not with that football. I just bought it six months ago. And 99 times out of 100, if we're in the backyard playing, her twin John is with us—plus my wife. If we're outside, then we all tend to be outside.

Sam's memory is complete, however, and her memory of that day, should it continue to hold a place in her mind, will ultimately become the memory of that day. Maybe she'll even write about it.

I keep thinking about my memory of nightmares that I may not have had and about playing catch on a day that could have happened but with a football Samantha and I didn't own yet...and when we wouldn't be likely to be alone, although it's not impossible.

Those two memories may be made up almost entirely from fiction.

I had nightmares as a child; I believe this because I still do, especially if I take something to help me sleep. But I also accept that I may be remembering only a single bad dream about kidnapping, something that resonated so loudly in my child mind that it has only gained in volume as it's echoed through the decades. My mother would have no incentive to lie to me about such a thing, and obviously she was older at the time and thus more able to remember. Given that my memory is of waking my parents up with my shrieking—in the middle of the night—I'd guess that it's the sort of thing a parent would tend to remember.

And Samantha is remembering real moments of the two of us playing catch in the backyard, but she's likely taken dozens of different days and formed a single, idealized memory that stands for the rest. When we play catch, it calms her. She has always enjoyed physical activity more than I did at her age, and I've likely played more football with her than I did with my own father (through no fault of his...I just wasn't an outdoor sort of kid). If a slightly warped memory of an event that didn't literally happen as she remembers it still brings her joy, then there's no call for me to get in the way.

Ultimately, neither Sam's memory nor mine does either of us any harm. But they point to the fragility and malleability of memory and to a fundamental flaw we all carry with us. Harvard's Daniel Schacter has identified seven "sins" of memory, and I won't walk through all of them now. Too much sin for one blog. His book's accessible, intelligent, and well worth reading. I'll walk through the one most relevant to families, to those of us who feel compelled to remember. One of memory's sins, argues Schacter, is "persistence bias"—the inclination we have to ruminate and obsess, especially about emotional memories. We go over events again and again, calcifying the narrative in our heads. We do this, sometimes, even if the narrative we impose only amplifies and intensifies the pain. We think about one specific point, one angry conversation or hateful comment or inappropriate public comment.

An authorial intrusion: The following paragraph felt unnatural to write, mostly because I wanted to tell a specific story about a specific relationship that ended badly. Apocalyptically. But there's no way to tell that story without embarrassing myself, my spouse, my kids, and a range of other folks who generally don't deserve to be punished for knowing a writer.

We tell ourselves the story about ending a relationship. The story cooks in our minds. We tell other people the story, altering details (highlighting some things more than others, deleting things that no longer seem relevant, probably making a few things up to add drama) to fit the audience. For one listener, we frame the memory/story as if we were victim. In another setting, we become an active, angry agent of change—probably one who knew the exact cutting comment to make for crushing effect. Which happens maybe three times in the average person's life. Probably not in the story we're telling ourselves and others, though.

But this is never, ever (hopefully) a matter of deliberate deception. It's just how our minds work. Some memories, especially the painful ones, stick. We deal with them by pushing on them and pulling at them persistently until we find some sort of balance…even if that "balance" is achieved by distorting the facts of what happened. (Academic postmodernists bristle at a word like "facts"—but I don't. Some things happen. Other things don't. Not all of reality is up for grabs, and not all perceptions are equal.)

Samantha tells herself the story of the two of us playing catch with our regulation NFL football on a perfect day last winter. This memory establishes its narrative rhythm through persistent repetition and sticks largely in that form for reasons beyond itself—for the happiness it brings her, I hope.

I remember my nightmares of being kidnapped, remember them coming night after night after night. If I'm right about when this may have happened, then it may have been somewhere in the wake of my older sister's death. If I was only seven or eight years old, I can imagine how my mind might have taken her sudden death—impossible to understand, then—and cross-linked to another fear that involved someone being suddenly gone forever: kidnapping.

I don't know if that's true. It could be.

It's my story, though, and I'm sticking to it.

It happens to everybody: You work away at something for a long time, forget to save the file as you go along, and lose everything when the system crashes. Or when the power flickers off for just a second. Or when your laptop battery dies. Or when your laptop overheats. Each of these things happens to me with some regularity, yet I have the nerve to be surprised. Always. Then I go through an abbreviated version of the seven stages of grief (mostly from denial to anger and, in the end, grudging, surly acceptance). Going through this process of loss repeatedly, though, really got me thinking about the things I do—and don't—save.

Save, Saving, Saved
April 2014

IN 1994 I was a graduate student at Eastern Washington University, writing my thesis on Norman Maclean. My computer was the first of my adult life—a replacement for my Brother typewriter, which was itself a replacement for my Commodore 64—a Macintosh Quadra 650.

It came with a monitor and printer, cost something like $3500, and had a massive hard drive: 350 megabytes. "You'll never need more memory than that," I distinctly remember the skinny, redheaded salesman saying to me. I could hear the stress he put on "never."

He was wrong about the memory needs I would have, of course, but he got one thing right:

"Make sure you save all the time. It won't crash a lot, but it will crash." Nothing was stressed in that pair of sentences, though.

I'm sure I nodded in agreement, and I'm sure all I was really thinking about was getting home and playing Sid Meier's Pirates. I know I didn't listen. Not down deep where it would have mattered.

That Mac did crash, only hours after I got it home. I was...predictably enough...sailing my pirate ship across a weakly pixelated

Caribbean Sea when it happened. I called the salesman to ask for help, and he told me to push the reset button. The reset button on the front of the machine. The button marked "Reset" in pretty good sized letters. He mentioned that the manual also contained this information, and I ignored the sarcasm.

Months later, the Mac crashed again, and I lost more than some ill-gotten gold. Somehow, I'd managed to write an entire chapter of my thesis—something about Maclean's ideas on lyric poetry and tragedy in King Lear as they applied to his own famous novella—without ever saving the text. It must have taken me hours to write those twenty pages or so, consulting my notes and my marked up copy of *A River Runs through It and Other Stories*, typing ideas in busts of key clicks, moving back and forth as the analysis developed. It would have been a long, long project.

Writing like that always was. Half a day, I bet.

And I never pushed the "Save" button once. Not one time.

The Quadra 650 crashed, taking with it a chunk of scholarship I tried to rewrite at one point but abandoned. Memory tells me…twenty years later…that that original writing was awesome.

Maybe. Probably not.

Foolish or tragic, I learned a horribly painful lesson about saving things. When it came time to work on my dissertation, five years later, that lesson metastasized into a full-blown disorder. For months at a time, I was terrified of losing anything, from a full chapter down to a fragment of a sentence.

Saving all writing became a compulsion. I emailed chapters to myself. I saved the entire work (a couple hundred terrible pages) on 3.5" disks—it took two—and bound them together with rubber bands. Then I stowed disks everywhere, in case my computer crashed or was stolen. I put disks in my briefcase. I put them in my desk at work. I put them in a baggie in the freezer (although, in my defense, I was advised to do that by a senior colleague, someone who kept a typed copy of his dissertation in his own freezer fifty years earlier). A few days ago, I found two disks, carefully labeled, in the glove box of our car. Fourteen years after I put them there to keep that written work safe.

I still save everything, and I still suffer the occasional loss. I had to do a factory reset on my laptop last summer and lost all of the records for an internship program I was developing. It happened while I was on vacation, but, thankfully, the total loss of that work didn't occur to me until I returned home weeks later.

But the compulsion to save everything leads to some odd essay fragments, like this one I found, maybe nine layers deep, in a 1TB drive smaller than a pack of cigarettes (about a million megabytes larger than that sad old Quadra 650):

March 28, 2005

> I'm holding my son; he's eight days old, and he just tricked me. He ate 10 CCs, hinted that he might eat more, and then refused. This is, I suspect, a baby's joke.
>
> It frustrates me, worries me, and scares me. These reactions happen all at once rather than sequentially.
>
> I'm frustrated that he won't eat for me when he'll eat for my wife. I'm worried that, if I can't feed him in the NICU, then he'll quickly starve when he comes home.
>
> My fright is related to this last worry. I'm afraid he won't eat for me, afraid he won't eat at all, afraid he won't gain weight, afraid he won't be healthy.
>
> I can't decide who'll come to my house first, given the starving state of my son (as I imagine it): Child Protective Services or the Police Department.
>
> Either way, it'll make a great prime time news docudrama. Stone Phillips will narrate.

I have the vaguest recollection of this—the anxiety attached to something as simple as feeding my son (and my daughter, since they're twins, and neither ever really ate any better than the other). But I fed the kids night after night, trying to take on as much of the feeding schedule as I could, since my teaching schedule was a lot more flexible than my wife's workday.

I put an enormous crib in my home office and fed them every two or three hours, watching movies while flat on my back on the floor. Heat up that many bottles, sometimes tired to the point of incoherence, and Stone-Phillips-based fears went away quickly.

Worrying is still second nature to me—first-nature, maybe—but that particular mix of frustration, worry, and fear is largely foreign, like an emotion that someone else experienced and then told me about. At the same time I found that fragment about feeding anxiety, though, I found this more developed piece, something that had already gone through several drafts (all saved carefully in the same folder):

June 22, 2006

>*While we've waited for the appointment with the specialist, I've watched Samantha's world get smaller. She spent her first Christmas climbing on the presents and pushing the biggest of them around the room. In January she was taking on her first words, starting with a loud shout of "Da-Da." When her brother began to walk in February, she followed him with her eyes but not her feet. He mastered "Da-Da" and moved on to "Thank you," "Hi," and "Touchdown," while her tiny voice got bigger so she could hear it. John began moving further and further away, even walking from the car to the daycare door on his own each morning, while she stayed at my side, always keeping me in sight if not within touching distance.*

>*The doctor told us that his grandchildren, all five of them, just left after a long summer visit, but I was skeptical. He looked old enough to have five grandkids and had the pleasant smile of a slightly goofy grandfather who sends the kids checks on every birthday and Christmas, but his declaration sounded too much like the kind of thing a car salesman would say to become my friend, all questions and exclamations masquerading as facts:*

"*What? You're from Montana? I spend every summer fishing in Montana!*"

Still, he's managing to contain Samantha's fifteen-month-old squirm with his left arm while simultaneously peering into her right ear. He's not even sitting down. This display of grandparenting skill puts me at ease, a calm he shatters by telling me what I already know.

"If she took a hearing test today," he says as he returns the light-pen sort of thing to his breast pocket and begins tickling Sam behind the knees, "she'd fail it for sure in the left ear, probably in both." Still holding her, he begins explaining the situation, pointing to various diagrams on the poster tacked to the inside of his office door.

I nod a lot but can't listen well. I want to hold my daughter but think it would be rude to take her away from this man she just met and clearly likes. My wife had tubes in her ears as a child, ten times, in fact, so I know most of the details already. Know them as well as I want to. As the doctor talks about fluid buildup and adenoids and clear liquid the color and consistency of honey, I think about Sam, now smiling and grabbing at his shaved, trustable face.

She was going deaf. I knew this before today's talk of fluids and ruptures and scarring that may not lead to permanent loss.

The doctor and my wife talk about her tubes and advances in the technology of tubes over the last thirty years. He shows us the tubes he'll install in Sam's ears, two bits of plastic smaller than salad pasta. Looking at them on his palm, I think that I could swallow them and not even realize it. Thinking this, I swallow reflexively around the dry lump in my throat.

He asks if we have questions, and I don't. My wife's in charge of asking the things that must be asked. Instead of questions, I'm haunted by an image of my daughter that I haven't seen yet, an image of Samantha tiny and unconscious and spread out alone on a white hospital sheet.

I see this almost-image every night, when I check on her and on John just before I go to sleep.

In her crib, though, the sheets are pink, and there are stuffed animals all around. There, twisted like a comma, Samantha's not alone.

While I'd largely pushed this memory behind the mental curtain, the emotions here, which aren't talked about directly in any depth at all, happened. And I remember all of it. I can feel the memory in my chest, even, as I type these words and my heartbeat revs up with anxiety over surgery that was successful (both times it had to be done), surgery that addressed the problem and left Sam, now nine years old, with perfect hearing.

I also can't help but notice that I admit, in writing, that I frequently use nodding as a way to indicate attentive listening while something else entirely is going on. I've said so twice, just in this post.

Obsessively saving my Word files—and every digital picture, ripped song, etc.—leaves me with a 1TB hard drive that's so messily organized it's hard to believe that the file structure was deliberate. How many folders, I sometimes wonder, can one man possibly name "miscellaneous"?

But those Word documents—badly named and illogically organized—are worth having. I've written before in Gum in Your Hair about the value of DVDs and images of the kids…wondering when enough is too much. These drafts and fragments of nonfiction give me something else, something that presents the facts of the experience in those years better than anything else can.

Of course, I only find such material when I'm digging through one "misc" folder after another, trying to find something I may have written a dozen years ago—if memory serves—about Norman Maclean. Or maybe Sid Meier's Pirates.

When John and I went to Scout camp during the summer of '13, we came prepared. I thought. We went on a massive foraging trip through the Walmart in Butte, Montana, and two different sporting goods stores. Memory tells me I spent something like $300 on various bits of gear, from a new hiker's backpack to a compass and match case for each of us to carry. Disposable ponchos. Emergency blankets. Everything I could think of. Thankfully, the Scout Leader is smarter than I am. He brought cases of water. Bug spray. Sunscreen. It was the first time in my life that I ever, ever felt like some bizarre "city slicker" sort of figure. (More honestly, I just felt like an asshole.) The Leader saved us, though, and John and I managed a few days of camping in peace. We found ourselves using the term "radically rocking awesome" to describe our time together. Time. Something I never seem to spend correctly. But I am always on the lookout for a way to talk about ancient Greek...

On Time
May 2014

I LEARNED THINGS last summer. At camp with my son, I learned that "This is a repeat after me song!" is the most aggravating sentence that can be spoken aloud in the English language. On that same Scouting outing, I also learned that sleeping shoulder to shoulder in a green Army surplus tent will protect you from wolves, especially when there aren't any wolves to begin with.

But mostly I relearned the lesson of time.

For several years, I taught ancient history—Greece through Rome to the Arab's loss of their Spanish empire. This involved teaching a lot of non-English terminology (Latin, Arabic, and Greek). As I lay in my Army tent, listening to the mosquito repellant buzz and smelling suntan lotion in the dark, it was the Greek ideas about time that my mind kept drifting to (partially to keep from focusing on the heat, which was almost intolerable). The ancient Greeks had two ways to think about time, one a lot more useful than the other.

"Chronos" referred to chronological time, that time that proceeds from one minute to the next until the minutes pile up into hours, days, months, millennia. This is the sort of time American culture pounds into everyone. Just today, I've asked "What time is it?" maybe four times since I woke up, and it isn't even noon yet. I have to ask, though, because I don't wear a watch. More than a decade ago, I was teaching at a Jesuit university where there were no clocks in the classrooms. So as my students would speak, I would glance down at my wrist to see how close the end of class was. I realized how rude that must seem, though: My students were talking, and I was glancing down at my wrist, like I couldn't wait for them to be done. So I asked them to keep track of time for me and never worried about it again.

As if I needed to ask students to pay attention to when class ends.

Chronological time is the enemy of family time, though, with its hypersensitivity to the way in which one moment leads to the next.

When we travel together, I obsess over where we're going and how long it'll take to get there. I look constantly at the clock on my dashboard and compare it to the miles we've rolled. I worry about when we need to check in at our hotel. I worry about dinner reservations and bedtime and whether or not I miss the television programs I enjoy.

I worry about chronological time. Too much.

As I lay in my tent, my son sleeping next to me, I thought more and more about the other concept for time that the Greeks possessed: "Kairos." Aristotle gave this term a very specific meaning, saying that it meant "fitness for the occasion" (meaning that a public speaker had to craft his/her message to fit the moment, the place, the audience). But the term was, outside Aristotle's study of rhetoric, a much bigger idea.

In ancient Greece, *kairotic* time was open ended. It was time that didn't care about the minute by minute progression but instead about the destination.

Kairotic time isn't about this moment leading to that one. *Kairotic* time is about what the moments mean. It's about the quality of the time spent rather than the quantity. While chronological time is determinate and specific, *kairotic* time is indeterminate and non-specific.

Last summer's plans were made with chronological time in mind: trips to see my parents, three camping trips, a vacation to the Washington coast, etc., etc., etc. Planning it all, I added up the mileage and shuddered at the amount of time I'd be spending in the Jeep between May and September. I broke down the number of days my son and I would be at camp and wondered how often I'd be roped into activities I resist and resent—like singing along, in a repeat-after-me song, about bears in tennis shoes. I calculated the number of days we'd have company sleeping in our home and looked sadly at how few days there were between company leaving and work beginning.

I worried over the chronological time of last summer for more than a year, worried it like a dog on a bone. When two members of my department suddenly resigned, leaving me to scramble to fill their positions only a month before classes started again, the summer's sand slipped through its hourglass even faster.

Find a picture of the Greek Titan Chronos out there on the web. It was like I could feel him breathing over my shoulder. Seriously, find a picture. Creepy. Like Zeus mated with Death.

But all that worrying—well, most of that worrying—over chronological time came before summer even started. That night in the tent with my son, though, I realized that something unexpected and unplanned had happened: *Chronos* had given way to *kairos*. Spending hours with my family—immediate and extended—shifted me from an obsession with the quantity of time to the quality of the time.

It felt great.

My kids attend church with their mother, while I worship at the Temple of the NFL. Or simply the Temple of Syndicated Television,

during the off season. When Elizabeth was away, and John was sup-posed to be an altar server, he sent this note to the priest:

Dear father,

I'm sorry I can't serve today I just can't do it without my mom.

Shame is a useless emotion, yet it's the one closest to hand when I lie on my back in the dark, waiting for sleep to come. Sleep has never come easily for me, and I've likely read thousands of books between the hours of midnight and four o'clock. In recent years, I've done less reading and more watching of Breaking Bad, Rome, Dexter, *and a whole series of even more questionable fare. The viewing helps keep the shame out. But shame's also what I turn over in my hands while I sit on my deck, in the late summer evening, listening to my sprinkler splash water against the fence, watching the sun set redly in Montana's smoke-filled burning season. I'm not ashamed of anything about the life I've lived, although I could have thrown down fewer beers, taken out fewer student loans, and chosen an early path that wasn't a major in Alcohol Abuse (with a double minor in Bad Decisions and Inappropriate Women). I carry no baggage from the first two academic jobs I held, although there were times where I allowed myself to be treated badly by those who had power over me. I am a man of probity. I think. But I am ashamed not to be a better husband, better father, better provider. It's a question of money.*

You Promised
June 2014

EARLY ON, MY daughter showed quite a bit of diplomacy for a 4-year-old. I first noticed it when she announced her career choice: "Dad, I want to be a doctor. For fat kids." That wasn't diplomatic, but her follow-up was: "I won't *call* them fat, of course."

Samantha continues to watch medical programs—anything that involves people coming to the ER. Her favorites are the stories that involve (a) people coming back from the tropics with a worm growing inside them and (b) people somehow managing to fall down a hillside covered with cactus…naked. (That seems to happen a freakish number of times, if reality TV can be trusted…) Rarely does she turn something off because it's too graphic. She's still thinking about a career in medicine, five years later, but now she may be a veterinarian.

I'd never encourage her to be a lawyer (unless she expressed interest in jurisprudence, of course), but she's already got a lawyer's sensibilities. I first noticed this yesterday, as we transitioned into lunch: "Sam," I said, "do you want six chicken nuggets or eight?"

She didn't even hesitate: "Six. I would prefer four, but apparently that's not an option."

Nice.

In eleven words, she demonstrated an understanding of Aristotle's division *topos* and the either/or logical fallacy. She knew that, logically, there was no reason she had to choose between six or eight nuggets. That was an artificial limit I was imposing on her, a rhetorical trick first labeled at least 2300 years ago. I didn't understand that until graduate school. When I was almost thirty. I'd planned on using that sort of argument on her for years, well into her teens. Apparently, I'll need to think of another approach.

But that was lunchtime yesterday. Today's lesson got me thinking about law school.

At dinnertime, we had an argument about the pace at which Sam (wasn't) eating. This happens from time to time. She's not a picky eater, not at all. She was confronted by a plate of oven-fried chicken, corn on the cob, Bisquick biscuits—green salad and sliced peaches on the side. All of these are favorite (or *favored*) components of a good meal.

The problem wasn't the food. Sam just wasn't in any hurry to eat… and time went by. A lot of time. Finally, I delivered an ultimatum: "You have ten minutes to finish. If you don't finish, you're losing your Kindle for tomorrow."

Done and done, I thought, brushing my mental hands together with smug satisfaction. Crisis handled. Disaster averted. This was the sort of clear action-and-consequence sort of thing I'd always been told to do. No general statements about "being punished" or something…just a clear statement of what's going to happen and why. Everyone else finished eating, and Sam was left alone at the table, picking at her food.

Twenty-seven minutes after my ten minute deadline passed, Sam finally finished her meal. I thanked her for finally doing a good job of cleaning up her plate, but I reminded her of the consequence.

She flipped out. Flipped out. There was shrieking. Apologies were proffered, and I thanked her for that, too, but noted that "sorry" didn't change the situation. Begging was involved. Tears flowed. She stomped her feet in frustration (but didn't slam any doors, since she knows the punishment for that is to open and close the door twenty times…fully open and fully closed. Try it. That *sucks*.)

Then the lawyer came out.

"I told you there was going to be a consequence."

"No, you didn't."

"Yes, I did. I told you what you had to do and what the consequence would be if you didn't do it." I find that I speak slowly and in very complete sentences when I argue with Sam. It's all that keeps me from caving in and doing anything at all to make the craziness stop.

"You did. But you didn't tell me what itty-bitty consequence it was going to be!"

Even in the moment, I had to admire how adroit she was on her mental argumentative feet. She was making a this-punishment-doesn't-fit-the-offense argument. But she was doing something else, simultaneously: Like any good lawyer, she made a point, and, when she had to abandon it, she did so by agreeing to half of what I was saying…while still keeping the no-Kindle-tomorrow debate alive. If I hadn't been so certain of myself, I might have waffled.

I *did* doubt myself. A little. For a second.

From the very beginning, though, my wife and I have taken a firm stance: We don't negotiate with emotional terrorists.

I shrugged, repeated that she's not using her Kindle tomorrow, and walked away.

Now she's lying on the floor, watching television (as the Indians slap the Mariners around for a while, at least in the first four innings).

All's right with the world, all dinner-related tantrum-inducing matters forgotten.

If her lawyerly tendencies stopped with dinner and Kindle denial, I wouldn't ruminate on it. But a different topic comes up every few days: going to Disneyland next summer.

She has cousins who go frequently. A handful of their friends have gone. Sam knows she wants to go, too.

I know other things.

I know that Disneyland is more than a thousand miles from Dillon, Montana, and that gas costs almost $4 per gallon. Our Jeep gets maybe 28 mph.

I know that we'd need to take two days to get there (and two days back).

I know we'd spend at least three days in that particular happy place and that tickets cost (according to a terrifying bit of web surfing I just did) over $900 for this particular family of four. That's on top of more than a thousand dollars to cover hotel expenses, plus meals.

I know I am not in that sort of tax bracket.

Sam knows no such thing, but she is convinced of something, and she keeps repeating it: "You promised."

Those are the two words currently committing domestic violence on my heart.

Sam's convinced I promised her a trip to Disneyland next summer. I have no memory of this, and it doesn't sound like anything I'd do. I promise only what I can deliver...or what I think I can deliver, anyway. I have zero faith in my Disneyland-in-twelve-months-going ability.

I can hold firm when Sam doesn't eat dinner and loses her Kindle. Action, consequence. It's tough to fight through, but I can do it.

My *promise* is different. I'm an English professor; it's not like I can pick up extra nightshifts and make some overtime. My eleventh book will come out this year or early next; the previous ten haven't changed my income bracket, so I'm letting history guide my expectations here. I write magazine articles regularly, but anything that pays by the word is, by definition, not a game changer.

When Sam reminds me of my promise, part of me wants to pointlessly rethink my career choices: professor, editor, writer. I've managed to pick three professions that I can (a) be good at and (b) still not make a dime.

"If you don't keep a promise," Sam told me last week, "then you're a liar." We weren't talking about Disneyland then, but the principle applies, I don't doubt.

I promised to take her to Disneyland next summer, even though I didn't promise anything. I'm just not quite sure how. Yet.

Tonight, Sam will go to bed; I'll read to her (currently we're on the third Percy Jackson book) for a half hour. She'll ask me to swaddle her tight in a flannel blanket that's covered in a weirdly disturbing baby duck pattern. She'll tell me she loves me. We'll make faces and giggle. We'll talk about the various monsters that live on "Dracula Drive"—a running joke kicked off last year by some reality show focused on American myths and legends.

Then I'll get to work, again, and pick away at my plans for the next year. There's bound to be something I haven't thought of yet, I figure.

And tomorrow Sam won't get her Kindle. She will eat her dinner with minimal silliness and at a normal pace.

I'll keep my promises.

I walked through my teens and twenties as if I were bullet-proof. My body was my amusement park, and I punished my liver like it was a disobedient stepchild. Aside from a few aches and pains, I just didn't feel like there was much wrong with me (aside from the fact that I couldn't gain any weight, no matter how hard I tried—not exactly a problem). Then my 40s rolled in, and my body went all Benedict Arnold. My doctor is great. I like her and trust her. It's not her fault that my good cholesterol is low, my bad cholesterol is high, and some of the other numbers found in my blood work are...well, wonky at best. Nothing's wrong, exactly, but some things aren't right.

New Normal
June 2014

I THOUGHT THEY were migraines.

For a year or more, in my early twenties, I suffered through frequent headaches, headaches so debilitating that my forehead was tender to the touch, and my right eye watered constantly. The pain was so awful that I would lie on my couch and jam a pillow against my head, cutting out the light and easing some of the hurt. If I could manage a nap, then I'd normally be alright once I woke up. A six pack of Budweiser (in bottles, not cans) would also do the trick, but I never mentioned that particular home remedy to my doctor—whose tests consistently revealed nothing. My wisdom teeth were all removed, working on the vague theory that maybe they were coming in crooked enough to be putting pressure on my jaw, causing pain to phantom into other parts of my skull.

Then they went away. For more than twenty years.

A few months ago, they came roaring back—same pain as before, the sort of pain that aspirin can't dent. They start in my left temple, radiate across my forehead and scalp and down my neck. My right eye first turns beat red and then runs.

They suck.

My doctor now is smarter than the doctor I had then, and she recognized "cluster headaches" when she saw them. They have all the markers of migraines, but they come and go, for months and even years at a time. I can't keep a refrigerator full of Budweiser to support my brown-bottle remedy, but I can take prescription medicines. I take one whenever I feel a headache coming on (although I'm reluctant to take one of these nasty chalk bombs because, even with insurance, they still cost $12 each). I also take a (thankfully cheaper) "prophylactic" medication daily, something that's usually for high blood pressure but also thwarts cluster headaches. (Until I was diagnosed by my awesome doctor, I had never heard the word "prophylactic" used in this context. I now try to work it into conversation whenever possible.)

Taking one prophylactical (I'm pretty sure I just made that word up, but I like it better than "prophylacticen" or "prophylactish," both of which occurred to me) medication daily and one at the first onset of pain is just part of the routine now. And those pills have joined a growing collection on my side of the shared medicine cabinet in the master bathroom. There are pills for my bad stomach and pills for my bad prostate. There are pain pills for my back, now that I managed to somehow herniate a disc this summer while taking a shower. A muscle relaxant works on the back, too, although stretching exercises work better. When I do them. Which isn't anywhere near daily.

All of this is part of my "new normal," I'm told.

New normal. It's a nice alliteration, but I hate everything else about it, including the fact that I've been ordered onto a "no starch, no sugar" sort of diet...because I somehow managed to put on twenty pounds in two months and (a) drop into a bad-cholesterol sort of category and (b) double the "safe" level of triglycerides in my blood. Both indicate potential trouble with diabetes and heart disease, but is it my fault that potatoes are awesome in all forms?

No chips, no corn on the cob, no rice. The new normal.

If my new normal only included dietary restrictions and prescribed medications, I could probably deal with it (although I'm spending an inordinate amount of time wallowing in a middle-age self-pity trough). But my new normal extends to my twins, John and Samantha.

As I write this, John's away at camp. We'll go get him tomorrow... after five nights away from home. He called us the first night (mostly just to touch base, I think, since he clearly didn't want to go home). He hasn't called since.

When he comes home, he'll learn something new: Starting two nights ago, we began to allow Sam to go to the local skate park with her friends...under no adult supervision. She's done well with this new freedom, an extravagance of epic proportions, given that months ago I was barely letting the kids ride their bikes around the block. (I'm a little over protective, alright?) John will expect this privilege to be extended to him, and it will be. Letting the kids go off with their friends is normal now...no matter how much it makes me sweat and fret.

It's quiet where I live, and the sound of kids laughing carries well in the hot summer air. Last night, while Sam was at the park with two friends (both boys, one sweet on her, I think) I sat on my back deck and read. I mowed the lawn in the afternoon, a big job that takes two hours and four beers (think of that as a preemptive strike on the next headache). Even better, I finally got my favorite sprinkler working. It's a green tractor with big, black wheels, and it crawls along 100 feet of hose, watering from my side yard all the way to the garden, finally fetching up against the swing set.

My son was enjoying camp. My daughter was enjoying her liberty. I was enjoying my book and the smell of cut grass and the fact that my favorite sprinkler was finally moving as it should be.

And then I realized that I have become a man who actually owns not just a sprinkler but a range of sprinklers—one of which is acknowledged as the favorite, the first among equals. Who has a favorite sprinkler?

Apparently that's part of the new normal, too.

As I finished reading to the kids tonight, John told me: "You and Mom are as good at reading as an owl with super glasses." That's a good thing, right?

I don't "write long," probably because I write so much as a freelancer now...in that 800-word-ish range. But I tend to write long far more often than I write short. Except here... It didn't take much to point out that I may have succeeded enough as a parent that I'm becoming pointless. As I should be.

Education for Irrelevance
October 2014

I WAS HAVING a good time, so it took a while for the reality of the situation to sink in. Like most parents, I'm not alone in the house much, particularly when there isn't some major chore ongoing, like mowing the lawn, which is, even on a cool day, a four-beer job with my ancient, blue-smoke farting mower from Sears.

But there I was, reclined in my chair, entirely alone, in the middle of a sunny summer Sunday. Elizabeth was on her way to Salt Lake City to see a specialist about her wrist. John was staying overnight with a friend. Sam was off at the skate park with her friend Tony who is, she assures me at every opportunity, not her boyfriend. I have my suspicions. Even the pets were in other parts of the house—Ike, our poodle, passed out in the sunbeam that beats its way across the living room floor every afternoon; Frank, our enormous long-hair cat, a feral we adopted in Nevada several years ago, sleeping either in my office or under a bed; Nora, a feral who adopted *us* a couple years back, off killing something smaller and weaker than she—part of which she likely would bring to me as a gift. Or possibly as a sort of cat-paying-rent business transaction.

I tried to find something engaging on television and couldn't, defaulting to a *Cops* and *Jail* marathon that could be ignored...or at least viewed only passively, between naps.

I cracked a beer but couldn't be bothered to finish it.

I didn't feel like reading—for work or for pleasure.

I found myself thinking about the ancient shark tooth I keep on my desk. It's five inches long from chipped tip to root, three inches wide across the base. Both sides are still surprisingly sharp, and the serrations can cut paper, even after the tooth sat in ocean-floor silt for a couple of million years. The Megalodon that hunted with that tooth in its head was centuries dead when my Montana home was still covered by an inland sea. He'd have been the apex predator of his day, though, whether we're talking millions of years ago or only ten thousand years ago, since this tooth suggests a shark longer than a full-size school bus.

Thinking about unwanted beer and skate parks and Tony-who-isn't-a-boyfriend and sharks as big as school buses, I was struck by the problem that I was experiencing. I felt restless, aimless, and bored. I was alone and didn't know what to do with myself.

There was nothing I needed to be doing, and no one needed my help with anything.

I felt irrelevant. My kids are nine years old. They have friends and can be trusted—more or less—to leave and then come back when they're supposed to; they have watches and know how to use them. They don't have cell phones, yet, but have a loose network of friends throughout the neighborhood, and they know who to turn to in the event of an accident, even if they can't immediately get ahold of me or their mother. They know how to reach me, both at home or by the cell phone I hate to carry and sometimes think I lose (albeit unconsciously) deliberately.

They don't need me around full time. They aren't *supposed* to need me around full time. And that's the point. I educated them enough to begin to make myself irrelevant.

It's a good thing, being largely irrelevant in these ways.

Still, it kinda ruined my Sunday.

John and Sam are playing with Legos on the far side of the room. John is dictating the terms:

John to Sam: "You have to be on a horse. No. He has to be on a horse. Turn him this way. He can have a shield."

Me (from across the room, watching the Olympics): "That sounds like a lot of rules, John."

John to me: "Could you please not interfere?"

Section II:
Background Noise

ROUGH DRAFTS, JOURNAL ENTRIES, AND

OTHER NARRATIVE FRAGMENTS

I am writing about a man whom I didn't like, and who didn't like me. It is consequently impossible to expect me to be fair.
—William Seabrook, *Asylum*

Colby argued that just because he had gone too far (he did not deny that he had gone too far) did not mean that he should be subjected to hanging. Going too far, he said, was something everybody did sometimes. We didn't pay much attention to this argument.
—Donald Barthelme, "Some of Us Had Been Threatening Our Friend Colby"

Shall I say that the container can not / contain the thing contained anymore? No. / Just that the lamb stew is leaking all across town / in one place: it is leaking on the floor of the taxi-cab, / and that somebody is going to pay for this ride.
—Alan Dugan, "Closing Time at the Second Avenue Deli"

Another Authorial Intrusion

My first thought was, he lied in every word.
— Robert Browning, "Childe Rolande to the Dark Tower Came"

WHEN IT COMES to Word documents, I'm a hoarder. I don't keep everything, but I seem to keep *almost* everything. On some level, I'm convinced that it's better to have a hundred copies than one, even if all of them are saved on the exact same drive.

We all compulse in different ways.

Until I started diggin' through the archives, though, I'd forgotten that my anxiety and fear about parenting…started long before I became a parent (and far, far before my mediocrity bubbled to the surface). My wife and I made the choice to pursue IVF despite its unavoidable cost and inherent risk. We made this decision in a difficult time:

I hated the job I had and was failing at it (or was being failed at it—the result's the same regardless of the verb choice). Our insurance (through my work and my wife's work) covered almost everything once Beth became pregnant, but it covered nothing before then.

We'd bought a house and turned it into a home. We even bought a dog.

I didn't want the dog. I hated spending hundreds of dollars on a poodle and resented the work he required just to maintain him in the level of comfort he demanded. The first time I took him for a walk, he nosedived off the curb, hitting the street face first and bending his neck in a terrifying range of directions. He went ragdoll. I thought

I'd killed him, and no one would have believed it was an accident, not after I'd made my feelings about him clear.

But Ike's sitting on my lap now as I write, his eyes growing dim with age but his neck thankfully unbroken. It was a mistake to dislike him so much at the beginning. It was a mistake to show my dislike at all. Things have worked out, though.

After first drafting this note, which I originally expected to be brief (note the title?), my inner editor said to cut that whole Ike-the-poodle digression. I resisted for two reasons. For one thing, this is the kind of writing I do all the time—wandering anecdotal bits that get saved on a hard drive for decades. For another, and I now warn my students of this fact on the course description I give them on the first day of class, I proceed by narrative digression. I can't think or write in a straight line; instead, I have to story my way from point to point.

Occasionally, I get lost.

Two years ago, in a history of technology class I was teaching for English majors, I suddenly realized that I'd been telling the story of the development of (and impact of) the AK-47 for ten minutes or more. I stopped cold: "Where the hell was I going with this?" I asked no one in particular. One of them prompted me back to the point I'd started with, and I tied the thing together. It worked out well.

I just did it again, starting with Ike and ending with my questionable pedagogical methods.

Anyway, there are no AK-47s in the journal entries, rough drafts, etc. that follow. There was one, an unpublished piece developed under the working title "Pot on My Penis," but I cut it. The story isn't even remotely about parenting.

Not that I always let that stop me.

As much as possible, the pieces collected from here on are organized chronologically, rather than digressively. I still digress a lot, but it's hard to write a straight line when bar fights come up, for example.

❖

Samantha and I often draw together. I keep this particular arachnid in my office...

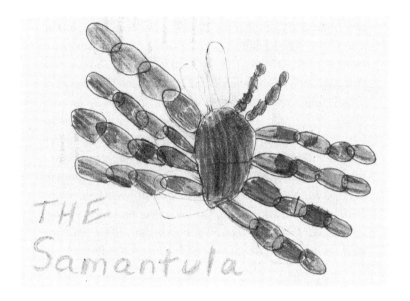

Throughout the IVF process, I never fully decided on my role. In depressing or stressful moments, I felt like the designated shot-giver and check-writer. But that was both inaccurate and unkind. When it comes to self-reflection, though, I'm rarely kind. I had a biological role to play, however...one that every boy learns by the time he's thirteen or so. The essay on that topic never completely came together, partially because it was, well, embarrassing. I can admit publicly to alcohol abuse, drug use, a wide range of poor choices in relation to jobs and friends and women. Apparently, though, I have trouble talking about masturbation. Two narrative scraps survived this confusing time—plus a move from Washington to Nevada, Nevada to Montana...and at least four major changes of hardware. I didn't know any of that was coming, though. All I worried about was making our life in Spokane work, not knowing that life wouldn't last much longer.

12-19-2003: Expecting Bad News

I EXPECTED BAD news. More specifically, I was ready to have the bad news I already knew confirmed. Elizabeth and I would have to adopt, and that would be that. The process would take years, and be very expensive, but that was what we had before us.

We saw a fertility specialist for the first time on the morning of December 19, 2003. His outer office smelled like carpet glue, and everyone apologized about it. Renovations, they said. He had a copy of my psychiatric records but didn't know why. Work stress, he guessed? We spoke with the doctor for maybe thirty minutes, followed by a gynecological exam that included an ultrasound of Beth's uterus. We spoke with a nurse practitioner about the process that was before us. The word *intercourse* came up a few times, but *masturbation* was never directly mentioned. We spoke with a financial consultant.

I think I asked questions when things were unclear, but I was reeling inside and developing a tension headache behind my left eye and in the temple on that side.

I expected bad news, so good news caught me flat-footed.

The possibility of successful IVF could be as high as 80%. Even 90% was mentioned once—so was 60%. Success stories were told. Perfect donor matches were discussed. Costs were nonchalantly covered, as if $15,000 were no big deal. The new Ford I just bought—just financed—cost nearly $6,000 less than these procedures.

And I don't have to jerk off for strangers to buy a Ford.

Beth began taking prenatal vitamins. We'll probably begin some time in October or November, some time after I have my summer teaching money. Beth wants to carry the child, and I want her to do what makes her happy, so there'll be no more talk of adoption.

Unless this process should fail in three attempts. Then we'll turn back to adoption, although we've not discussed this yet.

I ground my teeth all night in my sleep. Hard enough that Beth woke me up once. Hard enough that I woke myself up multiple times. My head has hurt all day. Hurts still, despite aspirin, ibuprofen, and migraine medication.

Mostly, I'm waffling between joy at the possibilities and pants-shitting terror over the stress this series of procedures will bring.

I worry about Beth's health. About Beth losing her job. About losing my job. About having enough money and time for a child. About having enough time to do the work that I'll need to get tenure. About having enough money to finish the basement—so we have a room for the child and for company.

About not being a good father.

At some point, I need to schedule a sperm test. Even the thought of this makes my dick shrivel. Go into a room. Jerk off. Into a cup. Give the cup to the nurse.

Sounds sexy…

And I'll have to do it at least twice—once for the initial test and once for the actual mixing with the donor eggs.

Maybe I should go to eBay and buy a *Playboy*—something that turned me on as a kid. Something with no complicated associations, aside from lingering adolescent shame.

Sometimes, I date a journal entry. Usually I don't. Such fragments and bits don't always paint the same picture of me (or the "authorial 'I'" or whatever) as is painted in the more polished, previously published pieces. This popped up eight months before my twins were born.

7-31-2004: Almost August

LESS THAN TWO hours left in July of 2004. My wife's sleeping next to me, on her stomach, bare to the waist. Her ultrasound is at 7:00 am, so we've set two alarms to make sure she's up on time. We've got all the medication and supplies, now that I picked up the syringes last week. I drank the last three beers in the fridge while I watched "Cops" and "Big Brother 5." Now Elizabeth and I are in bed, and August 1 is less than two hours away.

Everything changes in August.

Tomorrow, with the ultrasound, we officially begin the IVF process. I start my own medication on Tuesday. The actual implantation is in two weeks, give or take.

I'm teaching at Gonzaga for another week, but then summer session ends. It will be my last summer session at GU. Dave observed my teaching on Friday, and his letter of support will complete my updated placement file at The University of Arizona.

After that, it'll be fall semester and the job market.

I'm already homesick. I miss my living room, miss the open space, miss the silence. No TV in that room. Just bay windows, plants, and framed newspapers on the walls, headlines from the Great War, the attack on Pearl Harbor that thankfully didn't kill my grandfather (whose ship was in dry dock for repairs), the Lindbergh kidnapping. I love that room, and I'm already mourning its loss. And resenting the faculty whose actions have led me to this point. I'm not blameless in what's happened, certainly, but I don't own all of the mistakes that have been made.

But I'm the one that has to move on, and my wife—my family—is hostage to my actions.

"Shoot the Drift" was first drafted in August of 2005, as I sat in a classroom filled with beginning teaching assistants. They were there to receive a crash course in writing pedagogy—just enough information to get their feet under them before they stepped into classrooms of their own. A handful of them already had Master's degrees and teaching experience. Some of them would become my friends, particularly as I either directed their dissertation committees, taught them the history of ancient Greek, Roman, and Arabic rhetoric, or both. "Shoot the Drift" was the product of ten or fifteen minutes of work that morning. The essay was accepted for publication at Brevity...*but only on the strength of its first half. The last half of the essay needed significant revision. It's obvious why. Looking at it now, I see a wider window into how I was waffling at the time, though.*

Shoot the Drift: *Original Draft*
from August 2005

I'M ON MY knees in the dimly lit basement, gripping the pistol in my right hand, index finger on the trigger guard, left hand clapped over the right. There are six shells in the clip, loaded moments earlier by my clumsy, unskilled fingers, and I'm about to fire them in rapid succession into the target 45 feet away. My elbows rest on the battered brown leather surface of an old bar stool, where a long-ago tear has been covered with electrician's tape. I blink to clear my blurry eyes and bleary mind.

"Shoot the drift," Dave says from behind my right shoulder. He's telling me to compensate for the pendulum swaying of my arms and shoulders, the rhythm of my breath, the increasing beat of my heart. I've fired rifles before, many times, and Dave knows this, but the drift is different with a pistol. More pronounced. Dave will shoot after me, and he'll outshoot me easily. We know this before I pull the trigger for the first time. For now we aren't competing; he stands behind me and instructs, quietly and patiently: "Shoot the drift."

There's more here than instruction in marksmanship. Dave's delivered a lesson on accuracy in his three-word maxim, but he's also offered a startlingly accurate, inadvertent, description of the last year of my life along with a course of action for the future. Dave wears suspenders and sandals, hunts for pleasure, and reads Greek philosophy. He taught me to write and, later, taught me to teach others. He taught me to work successfully in academe and taught me to live life as an academic without subsuming my other senses of my self to the work. I'm not surprised that his counsel on pistol accuracy is applicable elsewhere.

"Shoot the drift."

I've drifted at work, ever since my administrative duties overwhelmed my love for teaching, ever since I stopped caring about keeping my job and instead focused on doing my job. I've drifted through conversations with several publishers, signing two new book contracts purely for the financial gain the work might bring and not for the eventual tenure such work could earn me.

I've drifted at home since Elizabeth and I began discussing adoption, reading manuals on the topic and consulting Web sites. I've drifted since we consulted with doctors about her Turner's Syndrome, a non-hereditary genetic disorder which only manifests itself visibly in her 4' 8" stature. When she was diagnosed at the age of twelve, the idea of never bearing a child didn't bother her.

She's not twelve any more.

I've drifted through the physical, financial, and emotional costs of *in vitro* fertilization, all of them significant. I've drifted through months of delivering Elizabeth's daily injections into her hips, shooting the needle in, pulling back to look for blood, plunging the oil-based hormone injection into her small body. She tells me the shots don't hurt, despite the ever-growing circles of bruises, blue-black at their centers and malarial yellow at the distant margins.

I've drifted beyond concerns about tenure, leaving my position as an assistant professor at a private school to pursue more meaningful work at a research university. In days, this professional drifting will uproot my family from our home in Washington and land us in Nevada

By this night on Dave's indoor and likely illegal shooting range, the children born of this drifting are less than four months old. My wife is now a mother. My parents are now grandparents. My closest friends, including Dave, are now aunts and uncles.

They're at ease in their roles. I am still drifting.

I begin to fire. The explosive smell is sharp and clean, a smell of chemical and machine working in faultless harmony. Dave cares for his guns and loads his own shells. I expect perfect operation from his weapon; I'm not disappointed. My shots come in an irregular rhythm, but they all fly true. This is a great surprise to me. I'd worried about shooting badly, about disappointing Dave, about putting a shot through his wood-paneled wall and into the gas line.

When I finish, I snap the safety, lay the pistol on the torn seat, check the target. We discuss the merits of various hits, mostly by pointing and shrugging with our hands, and Dave places an X across each with a black pen, marking it as mine. I rub my hands on the knees of my jeans, wiping away the greasy, fragrant smell of gun oil.

We resume our positions behind the stool. Dave lifts the gun, drops my clip to the floor, sets his own clip in place with a palm slap. He begins to fire. The shots are quick and methodical, the sound of all-business shooting. I don't need to see the target to know that the grouping is tight.

We pull the target free from the plywood and compare shots. I shake my head and shrug my shoulders at the same time, still rubbing gun oil on my pants—a gesture of combined nervousness, embarrassment, and respect. My shots look like a blast from a distant shotgun, pellets scattered at random across the cheap target's pulpy paper surface. Dave's shots overlap one another, no circle perfect because it intersects others. He sets the target on the barstool and rests both thumbs atop the grouping of his shots, covering them completely. The holes from my shots dance around his thumbs in an aimless, drifting sprawl.

I think about keeping the target but don't. My shots, at least, are nothing to remember.

My twins were born premature, just as I was. In 1970, being born six weeks or more premature was a potential death sentence. I was lucky. My eyes are terrible and always have been; over the years, I've had surgery on the muscles that control them half a dozen times, and my right eye still has a tendency to drift inwards. When my son asked me, "Why don't you get it fixed?" I just shrugged and said "meh." After RK surgery ruined my night vision back in 1990, I haven't wanted to go under the knife for any reason. John and Sam spent a month in the Neonatal Intensive Care Unit, though. Exactly a month. They were healthy, although Sam gave me a scare at her moment of birth. (I stayed safely hidden behind the curtain that ran across my wife's upper chest, separating us from the caesarean. When John hit the world, he gave out a shriek, and we were able to see him. Swaddled and cleaned a bit, Beth kissed his forehead. Sam came in silently and was whisked away by nurses so scared I could see the fear in their body language.) While in the NICU, the twins were almost always the only ones in their room. For a week or more near the end, though, they had a roommate: Sophia. She never made a sound. Something was cataclysmically wrong even before she was born, and her parents, roughly fifteen years younger than I, were terrified. My kids were healthy. Their kid was not. I couldn't carry the guilt that landed on my shoulders every time I saw them. Or her. Sophia.

10-6-2005: Guilt

THIS YOUNG FATHER wants an answer, something reassuring. He's maybe twenty-two and uninsured. His Sophia, less than a week old, is in the neo-natal intensive care unit, sharing a room with my premature twins. I'm standing in the back of the room, changing a diaper, trying not to interrupt their discussion with my presence.

"Well," the doctor pauses and shuffles through some papers on his clipboard. "It's either bleeding *in* the brain or bleeding *on* the brain." The young, uninsured father says nothing.

I shrivel inside and do my best impression of the invisible man. The invisible man changing a diaper. The invisible man changing a diaper and not eavesdropping on a conversation that's terrifying.

The doctor and Sophia's father don't look at each other. The father doesn't respond at all. They both just stare at Sophia's small, naked-but-for-a-diaper body. Tubes run out of her nose. An IV is taped to her tiny arm, a heart-monitor to her foot.

She isn't moving. None of us are moving.

"Well," the doctor repeats, "let's take her for that MRI."

They wheel her out together, not looking back at me and my totally healthy twins, and I feel something inside me loosen as the three of them leave the room. They'll be back, but maybe I'll be gone by then.

I'm going to try really hard to be gone by then.

Sophia. I can't stop thinking about her. It runs through my mind over and over again that her name means "wisdom" in ancient Greek. I can't stop wondering what it must feel like to hope that a child's bleeding is on, rather than in, her brain.

Both *in* and *on* are prepositions. I had to memorize a huge list of similar words while I was in the fifth grade, and I can still recite most of it by rote. That knowledge is almost entirely pointless, and neither is a good word in this context.

I finish changing John's diaper and swaddle him in a donated blanket that might have been pink once but is now the washed out color of generic laundry detergent. Samantha is still sleeping.

Both of them are healthy. Completely healthy. Arriving nearly six weeks premature had no impact on them—not on their lungs, not on their eyes. They're not even small, as far as twins go.

That's when the guilt hits me like a punch in the dark. I close my eyes, put one hand on each of my children's small heads, and sway slightly.

I feel guilty that they're so healthy and in the NICU, learning only the suck-swallow-breathe rhythm before they can go home. I feel guilty that their roommate is bleeding somewhere in or on her brain and having seizures and has young parents who don't have insurance.

The whole IVF process was overwhelming, but I didn't obsess about the cost or the danger nearly as much as I fretted about my required participation at the biological level. Well, ok, I did fret about money and danger, but I really stressed oddly and unduly about the part I had to play. With myself. Sad little pun intended.

IVF and Quality Porn
a partial draft

I'M THE FIRST patient to arrive at the office—so early that I actually have to stand outside in the cold, wishing for a pair of gloves, while I wait twenty minutes for the medical folks to arrive. My gloves are in my desk drawer on campus, where I always keep them, and I keep forgetting them because the weather warms up in the afternoon, and my memory is short. There's been a funeral at St. Al's cathedral every afternoon for the last few days, too, which is always distracting. My office faces the front of the church, so I grade papers to the soundtrack that follows Catholic death—bagpipes and tears, for the St. Al crowd.

There aren't many ways in which I can contribute to this whole IVF procedure, and I don't want to screw up the few opportunities I have. So I come to my morning appointment far too early.

I take the empty elevator to the empty waiting room, sign in at the top of a form that'll be full soon, and wait.

Nurses and receptionists bustle around, filing things and drinking coffee.

More patients arrive, all of them desperate looking couples who seem to carry their desperation like a scaling-fish stink that won't wash off their hands. Sitting in my waiting-room chair and passively reading a large-print edition of the newest *Reader's Digest*, I did my best to find distraction in military humor and a story of survival after a bear attack.

I sympathize with the mauled hiker. I know how she feels.

The nurse calls my name, and, by then, the waiting room is packed. Other people have been called, but always couples. When I'm called—a lone man—everyone looks at me. They know why I'm here and my wife isn't.

I've got a test to take.

I follow the nurse back into the depths of the office, fighting the urge to make inane small talk or stupid jokes that she has, I'm sure, heard before from other men in this awkward situation, this public performance of a teenager's private act.

We stop outside a wooden door. Set in the wall next to it is a metal panel, worn stainless steel that obviously slides to the left.

She hands me a cup, the kind of thing Nyquil is drunk from. I look down at it, gently squeezing its fragile plastic sides with my first two fingers, look back at the nurse.

She's not old—maybe only a few years older than I. Somehow, her age makes this even harder. She isn't pretty, either. I find myself disappointed by this. When a woman's about to tell me to jerk off, I want her to be sexy, not matronly.

"When you're done," she says, "put the cup in the metal cabinet. We'll grab it from this side. Any questions?"

How the Christ did I get here. That's my question.

I say nothing.

I nod.

I am struck dumb by small plastic cups designed to hold semen and liquid cold medicine.

She opens the wooden door and walks away without another word. It occurs to me that I should have asked for lubricant, but I'm not calling her back now. The brochure I read said I should ask for lubricant if I wanted it, but in no case should I bring my own. I can't imagine a situation that would include me packing KY in my jacket, ready to whip it out at any moment of need.

Until very recently, I couldn't imagine a brochure that included discussion of KY.

I shuffle through the door, a beaten man.

I was hoping the room would have mood lighting, and it does: a halogen lamp turned low, soft reflections off beige carpet and cream-colored walls.

I was hoping for a touch of class, and the oak cabinet holding the TV and VCR certainly fit my vague desire. A little too big for a 5'x8' room, but still classy in a not-bought-at-Walmart kind of way.

I was hoping the room might have a bed in it—something small and functional. Clean white sheets with a scratchy wool blanket. Maybe a couple of undersized hypoallergenic pillows, given that it's in a medical facility. There isn't a bed, though. Just two office chairs, a dark enough brown to clash with but not be offensive to the carpet and wall colors, and a small glass-topped table between. The place looks like a little waiting room, maybe a place an optometrist would have you sit while your eyes dilate. Comforting in a not-too-hot-not-too-cold way.

The sign above the TV cabinet, white with blue letters, detracts from both the décor and the deliberately peaceful atmosphere: "Alert Employees if Room Must Be Cleaned After Use."

My true disappointment is with the low quality of the porn.

The wire rack bolted to the wall has room for only six tapes. Five of the slots are filled, and as I read the titles from top to bottom, I wonder if someone organized them this way on purpose: *Crystal Balls*, a blank space, *Seven Deadly Sins*, *Sister Snatch II*, *Back in the Pink*, and *Chocolate Swerve #4*.

Like the room décor, the porn films just aren't what I expected. I was thinking Cinemax After Dark stuff—light on the plot, heavy on the seduction, long on the sex (but minus hardcore closeups and moneyshots). This all looks pretty hardcore, judging by the lack of any pictures at all on the films' boxes. Just colored slip-cases—mostly black, except for red *Sins* and, predictably enough, brown on *Swerve #4*—with titles.

I choose *Crystal Balls*, thinking that its place atop the stack might argue that it's the softest of this hardcore group.

When I attempt to put the tape in the VCR, another tape is already there. I hit eject and watch *Diamond Double XX* slide into view.

Knowing that the last patient in this room beat it to *Diamond Double XX* makes me want to leave. My stomach rolls over as I suddenly imagine what this room might look like under black light. I don't even want to touch the tape to take it out of the machine. I stand motionless for nearly a full minute, just going over my nonexistent options.

I put *Crystal Balls* back in the rack and wipe my hand on my jeans. So much for the films.

The magazine selection isn't much better: A Playboy from October of last year; a Playboy Blondes, Brunettes, and Redhead special issue; and a Hustler with its pages creepily stuck together.

I open the Playboy BBR randomly. I reach for the cup. I struggle not to burst into ridiculous tears, but apparently medically mandated masturbation depresses me.

This is not about my children. It's not about IVF or parenting. I stumbled across it in a folder of scrap files, aborted essays on Vietnam War literature and tentative outlines for uninteresting books on the teaching of writing. It's about memory, the questionable bedrock for so much of what I do, personally and professionally.

2005: The Teaching Life
an unfinished draft

I DON'T PAY much attention, so things go right by me. Students answer when I call their names, and I look at them, nod, and move to the next name. I'd be hard-pressed, most of the time, to remember who I just nodded to. The same kid could say "here" twenty-seven times in a row, and I wouldn't mark anyone absent at all.

This lapse of memory—chronic and continuous—makes me sound hyper-polite. A student raises her hand: "Yes, m'am?" I say. Male students are, of course, "sirs."

I've never had a mind for names, so it seems entirely right and proper to associate my terrible memory with my work: I teach and have a terrible memory. The two are inextricably bound.

But they support one another, too.

I don't pay much attention, so things go right by me when they happen. But I write about them when I'm writing with my students. I've taught memoir writing, in one form or another at one level or another, since 1993. I've simultaneously held my life at arm's length and made every effort to present some version of it to my students. A clean, sanitized version of my life—something with less profanity and more good decisions.

I remember teaching, although much of it blends together. I forget what class a student was in, then what year the student was in any class, then (sometimes) that the student was ever actually a student of mine. I remember their faces long after their names have faded, although sometimes a name will float immediately to the surface when I bump into a random student in the coffee aisle at Safeway: "Hey, how ya doing (slight pause, name floating to the top) Bill." Or maybe it's "Bill?" with a slight question-like lift at the end, just in case Bill is actually "Floyd" or "Rodney" or "Whatever just not Bill."

I remember teaching because it's the only constant. It's the thread that weaves my adult life together—and since it connects so seamlessly with my life as a student, I can follow it back to my early childhood at Beaver Dam Elementary. Seriously. A made-up name wouldn't be that stupid, for fear of sounding false. Beaver Dam. Then there was West Elementary, which doesn't exist any more. Neither does Beaver Dam, actually. One's been torn down, the other renamed. Doesn't really matter which met which fate. Then Junior High. Did the school even have a name? I'm not sure that it did. Anaconda Junior High? Maybe. It's still there. Maybe it still has the same name. Then Anaconda Senior High, home of the Copperheads. Of which I was not one. I was in photography, though, and took pictures of the various incarnations of the Copperheads—from football season to basketball to golf to track to whatever else I could take pictures of as a way of getting out of school.

Then came Eastern Washington University, where I literally made the transition from student to teacher. The first class I took was an introduction to literature, and I guess I chose my major that first morning of college. Maybe I should have shopped around. After EWU was Arizona, after Arizona Gonzaga, after Gonzaga Reno.

Somewhere in there I bought a cat. Actually *bought* a cat. Money on the counter. My father still mocks me: "Who pays money for a cat?" He's got a pretty good point. But like picking a major, I just decided I had to have a cat immediately. No one had any free cats then, so I bought one. A while after the cat came along, I got married. I had a roommate for a while before I got married, then had my own apartment, then another apartment, then rented a duplex with my fiancé. None of those things were part of any chain of causation that led to any of the other things. Just a chain of digressions.

I drank a lot of beer during these years, nearly two decades worth. Budweiser in a bottle was my favorite, but I'd drink Schmidt (even if my roommate and I had to put it in the freezer and do shots of moonshine first in order to choke such shit down). There was rum, sometimes. God knows what else. I think I drank Boone's Farm, mostly strawberry, which is odd, since I hate strawberries. I seem to remember buying a lot of boxes of red wine from a blonde clerk who thought I was 21 long before I truly was. She was pretty and flirted with me openly. I couldn't ask her out, though, or she'd learn my true age.

For a while I had a swimming pool to clean and, around that same time, I learned how to fix a swamp cooler. I earned various degrees and didn't care enough about them to go through the graduation ceremonies. They were a means to an end, a path leading to work far less physically demanding than that done by any of the men in my genetic makeup. I had a bachelor party and threw one for my best friend. These events were maybe five or six years apart, but both involved strip clubs in Spokane, Washington. I interviewed for a lot of jobs I never got and a few that I did. I got fired a little.

But always there was teaching and my bad memory.

My daughter, Sam, tells me she has five fears: 1. Spiders. 2. Bugs. 3. The Dark. 4. "People who say 'Gollum' a lot." 5. People who stand in the dark where you can't see their faces and say "Gollum" a lot. None of these fears seem unreasonable to me.

I write about my memory a lot...because I write a lot about my memories. I don't think I've ever crafted a deliberate piece of fiction while calling it nonfiction, but personal and professional knowledge tell me that fictions must regularly occur. On the personal side, I know that I have a bad memory. I just do. Random things make it into the permanent storage bin (like the time my father had to have our septic system pumped...and needed to pull me aside to tell me that when you have a septic system, it's not a good idea to flush condoms down the toilet). And things that should stick just flash right by (like remembering my sister's birthday, which might be in April, although I'll have to check). On the professional side, my inner writer knows that the very process of crafting a story makes reality into something of a fiction. Stories have parts: Exposition to set the scene, Rising Action to ratchet up the tension, a Turning Point where the action meets its climax, Falling Action that drops into the Resolution (where all good stories have their clean end). Life doesn't have any of that until we impose structure upon it, and calling an event part of the rising action reframes the event, turns it into something it wasn't while it was happening. Worse, I know that some of the essays I've published (in Mistakes Were Made *and elsewhere) have been written and revised many times, sometimes over the course of a decade. I don't know how much I can craft a story...until it moves entirely away from the events that actually happened, without me even realizing it. The fragment below is another random bit of narrative that dropped out of an undated Word file. Since my daughter started wearing her Batman hat before she started kindergarten and only stopped halfway through the third grade, this could have happened in a broad stretch of time.*

A Terrible Remembery

"DAD," SAM TOLD me, shaking her tiny head hard enough to make the Batman stocking cap perched there tilt precariously, "you don't have a good remembery." This seemed like a pretty harsh judgment, given that my only failing was not remembering the name of Spongebob's nemesis, Bubble Bass. I apologized profusely, but Sam still muttered as she walked away: "Not a good remember."

Sam's right, of course. I do have a terrible remembery. It's a flaw I cover with humor, politeness, and a complete disregard for the feelings of others.

I never know how to end things, especially when it's an essay I've written pieces of over a long stretch of time. I first drafted "Peter Benchley is Dead" (I just typed "Dad" instead of "Dead"—Freud, anyone?) in the spring of 2006. I wrote it and rewrote it, adding sections and taking out details, tightening the narrative and re-braiding the organizational pattern. I sent it to journal after journal, and it was rejected every time. In the end, it was accepted for publication in Fourth Genre, *a top journal in the field of creative nonfiction. The editor wanted revision of the end, however, and I struggled. I wrote several versions across 2012, each worse than the one before. Ultimately, the ending worked only when I paired the text down. But these last two sections still speak to me, even though they had no place in that final draft.*

draft ending cut from "Peter Benchley is Dead"

THE NEWS IS on—what passes for news on CBS in the early morning—but I'm only listening with half an ear. The 2006 Winter Olympics in Torino, Italy, start soon, and there's some "women only" cruise going on, the kind of thing viewers wrote letters begging to get onto. These two stories, neither important, dominate the conversation I'm ignoring. Instead, I am feeding my son while his twin sister, Samantha, rolls on a blanket nearby, already fed and awash in her need to sleep.

We're sitting on the floor, facing each other, legs spraddled out to each side, the pose we sit in when we roll his racquet ball back-and-forth. I'm tipping the bottle of milk upwards enough for him to suck at the rubber nipple. He's not eleven months old yet, but he can normally hold the bottle for himself. Today, he feels like having his father do the work.

As John finishes his bottle, I hear something important rise from the palaver: Peter Benchley, author of the novel *Jaws* and one-time speechwriter for President Lyndon Johnson, is dead. I don't hear anything that follows, don't hear any of the details of where and how and what the commentator thinks this writer's life meant.

I pull my son into my lap and rock him.

Tears spill out of my eyes with a suddenness that startles both of us. I cradle John against my chest, and tears land on his upturned face.

He looks up at me and squints one eye into a half-wink. I wink back at him, swallowing around the deep lump in my throat.

"Peter Benchley is dead," I whisper.

The nightmares stopped when I moved my family home to Montana, although I obsessively prod my psyche with a near-constant diet of shark films delivered via Netflix. A copy of *Jaws*—the Reader's Digest Condensed Version from 1974—rests on my bookshelf, only a yard or less from where I write. Its cover is green and blue—a sort of floral pattern, like wallpaper in a grandmother's living room—and I keep a yellow bookmark on the image where a caged diver meets his brutal end. The album *Jaws of the Shark* is just upsetting enough that I keep it on a high shelf, above the line-of-sight of my twins, now seven years old and snugly dependent upon one another.

Neither the book nor the album is a survivor of my childhood. Both are products of late night eBay searches. I keep a fossilized shark tooth, another eBay acquisition, on my desk, although my twins sometimes take it to Friday first-grade show-and-tell. It runs almost three inches from tip to root, and I worry my thumb against it in anxious moments. I have to use care; after two million years of abrasive sleep at the bottom of the ocean, the edges are still serrated and slightly sharp to the touch. The shark that hunted with this tooth was dead and gone while my Montana home still held a large part of the North American Inland Sea. Once enamel white, the tooth has taken on the color of its geography and is brown from sitting for so long in shifting layers of sandy silt.

I visit Stacie often now, usually alone, standing stolidly over her grave, my great grandmother and great grandfather to the left, more distant relatives broadcast beneath other stones throughout this section. At sunrise, my shadow stretches out before me, blacking the names and dates.

I take my twins, John and Samantha, to visit their aunt Stacie, too, but rarely. Cemeteries are no place to fear, they should learn, but they are no place for the healthy to linger. They browse the stones, read inscribed words aloud. I teach them to show respect through whispers and carefully placed footsteps. I tell them stories.

Often, I take them to Georgetown Lake, even on white winter days when the weather argues that I shouldn't.

Trudging from our Ford to the lake's frozen edge, my daughter falls behind. Walking in deep snow is, like most of my life in Montana, new to her. Neither Elizabeth nor I notice, our faces tilted downwards to hide from the burning wind that's pushing across whiteness broken only by ice fishermen in their shacks. We huddle close together as we walk, huddle for the illusion of warmth and shelter proximity allows. She unzips my jacket slightly and slides her ungloved hand inside, resting her palm against my chest.

John is the first to hear his sister howl as both her feet disappear into the snow past the knee, leaving her to flail arms covered in a pink and polka-dot coat. Anything more than this will cause her to lose her balance or lose her boots. Her glasses flash, even in the subdued sun, and her black Batman cap blows off and out of reach.

As we watch, John returns to her one laborious step at a time, scooping up the cap and stuffing it into his pocket. He soothes her with words I can't hear, wraps her arm around his neck, leverages her free.

My eyes tear up in the wind, and I wipe my cheeks

Together John and Sam walk to the lake's crisp edge, supporting one another, leaving their parents behind in the snow and stillness.

I write a lot about my sister. More than I realized until I began to troll through my old files, some ten or even fifteen years old. At one point, I seem to have tried to begin a version of "Peter Benchley is Dead"—built around the many and varied old movies and television programs that make me cry. I didn't get far.

Easy Tears

BATTLESTAR GALACTICA MAKES me cry. I watch it with my children, and every foolish plot brings a lump to my throat, just like every repetition of the opening and closing monologues make me blink back the tears.

The pilot episode, first broadcast on September 17, 1978, came only two months after Stacie died. That summer comes back awkwardly, maybe because the first thing I remember is trying not to shit my pants at a funeral. Maybe because I don't remember the summer's second funeral at all. There was a wedding between those two funerals. My grandfather decided to dig a basement by hand.

There's probably a lesson there, maybe a metaphor. But all I have is *Battlestar Galactica* and a 7-year-old's memories of digging in the dirt and almost not shitting his pants at a funeral's after-party.

Being the father of a daughter, I sometimes stumble across a memory of my sister. It happens when events repeat, I think, some new experience kicking over a can and finding the same old experience underneath. It happened the first time when I was watching a DVD containing old episodes of Scooby Doo, my favorite Saturday morning show. Until Scrappy Doo came along and ran the whole thing into the toilet.

Dracula on the Porch

THAT NIGHT, MY sister and I lay on a fold-out couch on the screened-in porch, watching sheet lightning and smelling eastern Montana. We were at our Aunt Earleen's house together for the last time, although we couldn't know that. In the expectant, uneven spaces between lightning blasts, we spoke of Scooby Doo.

Stacie was twelve, while I was six, but we were united by our joy in that morning's episode: "A Gaggle of Galloping Ghosts." It had everything: Dracula, a Werewolf, Frankenstein's monster, a gypsy fortuneteller, and a castle moved to America from Transylvania, stone-by-stone.

The ending was a predictable victory by meddling kids, but the ending was entirely beside the point: Hours after watching the show, which first aired not long before I was born, we were still talking about the monsters.

Stacie loved blood, loved to build special effects of rubber and ketchup. I have pictures of us together, both of our faces painted to include livid bruises, swollen eyes, bloody lips and noses. Our hands, in one photo, are wrapped around each other's throats in mock strangulation.

Nearly every time I visited Aunt Earleen's ranch near Big Timber, I had some kind of accident. The gate to the side yard was especially predatory.

My nose exploded. I staggered backward, wailing in pain as my sister kept me from landing on my ass. Blood ran through my hands, down my arms, dripped onto the concrete walkway. Stacie wrapped her arm under my shoulders, holding me up and guiding me back to the house—where I would spend the next twenty minutes with my head tilted back, back so far it made my neck ache, and with a towel filled with ice pressed to my nose, neither giving aid nor comfort but stopping the bleeding.

Before it stopped, though, I sat on the closed toilet seat, head tilted back and one eye covered by a pink towel filled with ice, tasting the salt as my blood ran like snot down the back of my throat.

I don't remember if my sister stayed with me.

It seems like that matters.

A story problem my son wrote in 3rd grade:

Write a story problem for the number sentence **9 – 8 =** ☐ .

There were 9 zombeis, I shot 8. How many zombeis are left?

When my family lived in Nevada, from 2005 to 2010, I commuted 35 miles or so to/from work. Most of the time this wasn't an issue, and I was able to get home in time to see my kids. I used a digital recorder to "write," and I got pretty good at drafting things behind the wheel. The commute was all Interstate driving, and for the most part the road was plowed. But one night in 2005 was particularly bad, both because of poor visibility and a slick driving surface. Combined with some questionable driving.

Sliding on the Ice

IT'S THE FIRST day of classes following the Thanksgiving break. Some of the students aren't back yet—some of them are back but won't ever, really, be back to campus. One emailed to tell me he witnessed a stabbing at work and was being kept at the police station. A security guard at a casino, he stopped a drunk from climbing on stage to paw at one of the topless dancers. There was pushing and shoving. My student wasn't stabbed, but he was close enough to be splashed when his friend was slashed across the throat.

I suspect this guy won't be back to class.

The first snow flurries hit Reno today, and the ground is slick. When I leave my office, it's already been dark for more than an hour. The ground is slick with new snow, and I slide around on my leather-soled boots. It's time to bring out the biker boots that I bought during my second year at Gonzaga, the boots that make me maybe two inches taller and look very, very tough.

Before I can bother with wearing black Harley boots and feeling tough, though, I have to get home. And tonight, I can barely make it to the parking garage without falling down. Only a good sense of balance—and the fact that I'm carrying almost nothing in my backpack—keeps me upright.

Traffic's a mess, backed up for blocks. It takes me twenty minutes to get two blocks, and even then I'm still miles from Highway 395 south and Interstate 80 east.

The roads are icy now and still will be in the morning when Beth goes to Sparks for her ultrasound. Everyone is driving slow, aside from the semi-trucks and the SUVers. I'm averaging between 20 and 25 miles per hour, and sometimes even that's too much. As I pass exit 28, I get a good look at an accident. Cars facing the wrong way, lights off. No blinkers on or road flares anywhere. Seems like a bad situation that's set to get even worse. No police or highway patrol on scene yet and I don't stop. I couldn't. I was too busy sliding sideways and pumping my brakes as I went past. It's a terrifying moment, in a detached kind of way. It's not that I don't think I can die; I just don't think I'm going to die tonight. I'm sober, have been for weeks, and it's not even snowing. Plus, I've been in slides before.

I'm seventeen years old, and Jimmy and I are on our way back from the west valley. We had to get my girlfriend home before curfew, and the road conditions made that almost impossible. Water's coming down in steady sheets, turning the highway into a long and rutted lake, and lightning fires in every direction, silhouetting the mountains in the distance. The car hydroplanes constantly. Jimmy's driving with one hand, keeping time on his thigh with the other. Axe, one of our favorite groups, is singing on the tape deck, discussing Terry who, apparently, doesn't want to go back to the City of Angels no more. She's seen her fill of fallen angels. Enough for a lifetime.

We're both singing along with Axe when the front left tire blows out and Jimmy's red Ford goes into a skid. It slews back and forth, twists entirely sideways, then straightens out again, still fishtailing like crazy.

All we can see is rain reflected in the headlights.

All we can hear is Axe, moving from the closing beats of "Now or Never" into the opening piano riff to "Rock and Roll Party in the

Streets." If we were listening to the actual album, this'd be impossible. But this is a mix of our favorite songs in our favorite order. And that stinker "Video Inspiration" is nowhere to be heard.

Jimmy's one hand is still on the wheel. The other hasn't left his thigh.

As the car goes into another wild fishtail, spinning entirely around in a sickening 360, Jimmy looks at me. The looks seems to last a long time but probably doesn't.

With no trace of humor or horror, he says simply, "Hold on, Shane. I don't think we're going to make it." He enunciates each word very precisely, very clearly.

As the car spins back around, now only coasting and no longer fishtailing, we're stunned for a moment by this casual observation.

Then we burst into hysterical laughter.

We know our lives are in no real danger; we know that we could die. It's the paradox of being seventeen. We have girlfriends. We aren't drunk. Nothing bad can possibly happen to us. Not to us. Not now. Not yet.

I'm still fourteen miles from my Nevada home, not even halfway between Reno and Fernley, and traffic's still crawling through the snow. The Hummer in the left lane is going maybe three milers per hour slower than I am and won't move over, so I end up passing him on the right. It's the only way for me to get out of his blowback and improve my visibility. This seems more dangerous tonight than usual, and it always, always pisses me off. Passing on the right is illegal, no matter the reason, and this asshole is both putting me in danger and making me break the law.

Not that legality has ever been a major concern for me.

Elizabeth's ultrasound is tomorrow morning, and I hope the roads are better then. We still don't know why the ultrasound is even being done, don't know what test threw up a red flag. We weren't home when the clinic called to confirm the appointment, so we got a message instead of an explanation. And we don't have

Group Health anymore, so we can't get a doctor to call us back. Our HMO is less than loveable.

Ten miles from home the Hummer that was hovering just above my speed and blinding me decides to move over after all, sliding into the right lane without signaling and almost taking out the car behind me. This seems impossibly dangerous, but, at some point, even caution itself becomes dangerous. I've just passed the Derby Dam exit, and traffic is merging. Suddenly I'm part of a convoy, fumbling through the snow on roads not yet familiar to me.

I damn-near get rear ended by someone with a Nevada Wolfpack license plate. The car ahead of me is from Minnesota, according to its plate. Whoever's driving it should know how to drive in these conditions, but the weaving and waffling suggests he—or she—is as competent as a fourteen year old behind the wheel for the first time. Speeding up to 60 on icy corners. Slowing to 20 on dry-ish straightaways. If Minnesota flies off the road at some point, I'll be hard pressed to stop and check for injuries. Or survivors.

Once I get going in the snow, I'm reluctant to stop for anything until I get to my destination, even when continuing is almost a sure recipe for disaster.

I drove nearly a hundred miles—from Missoula to Anaconda, Montana—listening to the same Billy Joel album over and over again. It was "52nd Street." One of the worst blizzards of the winter of '89-'90 was blowing, and I'd been driving for nearly twelve hours already. I was still dating my last high school girlfriend and was driving back to see her, not knowing our relationship had ended months before. The signs were all there, but I forced myself to ignore them. I was too immature, inexperienced, and lust-blind to notice. Or to believe. For 91 miles, Billy Joel sang the same songs again and again while I followed the taillights of the car in front of me.

If she wrecks—and I assume it's a "she" driving, for no reason at all—then I'm doomed. I'll follow her off the road, into the ditch, etc.

Her lights are the only thing I have to follow. When semis blow past, I don't even have that. I have no clue what's guiding her, and I don't want to think about it.

I spend the entire drive thinking how stupid I am for leaving Missoula. For driving all day long. For being involved with a high school girl too young to ever wait for me, regardless of her repeated declarations and the absurd depth of my need. For holding on to a relationship with a high school girl who is, I know but won't admit, involved with multiple other men. And has been since before I ever left for college. Including Jimmy.

Billy Joel provides the soundtrack for all of this snow and the stupidity. I never take my hands off the wheel once to pop the tape out and to look for a radio station. I'm too afraid to let go of ten and two o'clock. I don't take my eyes off the road, either, even though it often doesn't matter if I look at the road or close my eyes all together. All white one way, all dark the other. I can't see a thing either way.

But keeping my eyes open at least gives me the illusion of control, just like the whole trip allows me to maintain the illusionary relationship.

I'm almost home now. Twice I've gone into terrible skids, the kind that send my heart into my throat and make my ass pucker. I was thirty years younger when Jimmy nearly wrecked his car in the rain. Age changes everything. Both times I steer into the skid, remove my foot from the gas, straighten the car, downshift, and move on. If driving on ice in the dark and obsessing about the past were a sport, I'd go pro. After winning a gold at the Olympics, I'd go pro, that is. I'm riding out these slides, and so far, everything's ok.

The message from the nurse—Gail?—said something chatty and non-threatening: "Hi. Just calling to confirm Elizabeth's appointment for Tuesday morning. Call us if you have any questions." We have a terrible answering machine, so there was a lot of static. Plus, our fax machine always wants to pick up, even when it isn't an incoming fax, so it beeps while the recorder does it thing. Like the two of them are arguing over who gets to answer. So the message was hard to hear over the static and the fax machine's beeping—and impossible to comprehend.

Call if I have questions? All I have are questions. Questions and lousy insurance.

At first, we thought maybe she was pregnant. Unlikely, given her Turner's Syndrome. But her period was late, and "unlikely" isn't "impossible." It would be just our luck to go through the difficult and expensive IVF process in order to get our twins…only to then have Beth get pregnant naturally immediately afterwards. Some blood spots and cramping disabused us of that theory, though. So now we're really in the dark, sliding towards an appointment we didn't know was scheduled and don't understand and don't dare cancel.

This is nothing new. We've been sliding for more than a year. Only now does it seem like we're coming out of it, starting to find our way as parents, starting to get onto our economic feet.

I pull into the garage, turn off the car, and close the door using the clicker on my visor. The bulb burned out in our garage door opener, so I'm immediately left in the dark. I sit behind the wheel, listening to cars go by on my street, then go into the house. My children are still awake, and they both smile when they see me. John begins rapidly crawling across the floor towards me—something he's only been able to do since yesterday or the day before. Samantha still crawls slowly, but she doesn't come at me, now. She knows that I'll come to her, which I do, scooping her up into my arms and blowing a wet, loud, raspberry of a kiss into her neck, just below the ear. John bellows loudly, holding himself up against the coffee table. He's the King of the Living Room, and he demands that I acknowledge him.

I do. By bellowing back in the same pitch and tone. We go back and forth several times. Then he gets tired of the conversation and crawls off down the hallway. I could have gone on for hours.

Elizabeth brings me a cup of hot tea—plain Lipton, with too much sugar. We follow our routine. There's comfort in the routine, a peace I never could find at the bottom of brown bottles.

I still look.

My son crawls fastest, so he is bathed first. He stands at the edge of the tub while it fills, straining his arms and, simultaneously, lifting first one leg and then the other—feeble, half-hearted attempts to kick a leg up and leverage himself into the tub, something he won't be able to do for at least six months. Once he's undressed, I lift him into the tub, where he immediately begins crawling back and forth, stopping periodically to smash his hands wildly against the surface of the water. This is a game he's learned from his grandmother, and it sometimes splashes water all the way into the hallway. Because of this game, the bathroom floor is the cleanest in the entire house; it gets wiped down every night.

John plays in the tub while I squirt soap and shampoo on this naked moving target as best I can. My aim's gotten better over the last few weeks, so I manage to get him clean while only wetting the front of my shirt and the sleeves, one to the elbow and the other nearly to the shoulder.

Eventually, I'll just start to take my shirt off beforehand. Like I do when I bathe the dog.

To finish John's bath, I lift him out, towel his squirming form off, take a quick swipe across his mostly bald head, and release him. Immediately, he crawls, nude, for the living room—where his mother waits with a diaper and footy pajamas.

I retrieve my daughter from the living room, where she's happily rolling around in the dog's toy box. Everything he has is either furry or squeaky, and she loves both. His toys are far more intriguing than hers. I carry her down the hallway, undressing her and dropping clothing as I go; by the time we reach the bathroom, she's naked, and we've left a trail of socks, sweat pants, and t-shirt, a trail that culminates in a wet diaper sitting on the floor beside the filled tub.

Samantha also loves her bath, and she flails even more wildly than her brother. Unlike John, her flailing has a rhythm: Slap the hands against the water three times, gasp for breath and blink because all the flying water has simultaneously blinded and muffled her, giggle and smile. Repeat.

Bathing my daughter after a terrible ride home in the snowy dark, I'm suddenly struck by a moment of recall so total it's almost time travel. She's splashing her hands madly in the water that's just a shade over lukewarm, holding a red plastic ring in her left hand and a vinyl book in her right, something about water that has a picture of a blue octopus on the cover. Water's flying everywhere, and she's trying desperately to reach other floating toys with hands she doesn't have free.

My work and my commute and my kids have kept me busy, so I haven't cleaned the bathtub lately. And Elizabeth doesn't clean the bathtub. Or the toilet. It's one of the absolute delegations in our marriage, and I take the tasks on willingly enough—just not always in a timely manner. She knows I won't fold laundry and doesn't call me on it. I know she won't clean the bathroom. It works for us, regardless of the why. I haven't bleached anything lately, though, and I suddenly see a splash of red growing behind the shampoo.

The stain I can see is slick-looking and slimy, the color of cheap gum or Mr. Bubble.

When I spot this stain, I'm trying to wash Samantha's thickening blonde hair with a small towel and am laughing so hard my sides hurt. She looks over her left shoulder and smiles, showing me the tooth that just cut through two days before. Bottom front. Her first.

I stop laughing when she smiles, and tears hit my eyes so hard that they throb. My head aches and pounds, and I can feel my heart beating in an ugly, irregular rhythm that makes me anxious and floods my mouth with the metallic taste of adrenaline, like I've just sucked on a dime.

It's the panic I didn't feel all the way home, not even when I nearly slammed into the Hummer, nearly got rear ended, nearly flipped while wildly spinning.

I'm bathing my daughter and having an anxiety attack, and for that instant I'm back in my fungus-filled, pot-stinking shower in 1993, back in the life of binge drinking, daily hangovers, constant and crippling loneliness and depression. The endless drive home stretched my nerves like a bungee cord, and they just snapped back unexpectedly, snapped back hard enough to leave a mark.

A mark next to all the others.

Then Samantha smiles and giggles, a smile so complete that her eyes crinkle half closed, and pounds her fists into the bath water. She loves her nightly bath, the time with her daddy.

I smile back.

When I first got onto Facebook, I never wrote "I" before anything; instead, I just let the name on the page stand there in place of the pronoun. But this is what "Shane Borrowman" heard his son say, perhaps at age five, indicating a shared future of zombie movies and games:

just heard his son assert, with some authority, "Zombies hate walruses." Nice.

In "Sliding on the Ice," I mention the terrible, filthy shower in the apartment I shared with my best friend in 1992 and 1993, just as I was finishing my teaching degree and preparing to start my Master's Degree in American literature. The horror of that shower is impossible to remember without a shudder. I include it here because it is, in the end, one of the clearest places where I can look at the often-depressed young man I was and the sometimes-troubled middle-aged man I've become.

A Red-Stuff Moment, 1993
drafted ca. 2005, revised 2013

This is one story I've never told before. Not to anyone. Not to my parents, not to my brother or sister, not even to my wife. To go into it . . . would only cause embarrassment for all of us, a sudden need to be elsewhere, which is the natural response to a confession. Even now, I'll admit, the story makes me squirm.

—Tim O'Brien, "On the Rainy River"

SOMETHING RED GROWS in the bathroom, a mold or moss or fungus the color of spilled grenadine. The red stuff takes up half the floor in the shower stall and is showing in the sink, moving outward from the flange. It's growing in the toilet, at the water line, and on the porcelain base's urine stained sides. Chalky blue Comet will not kill it, even mixed with bleach.

I shower here every morning before pouring on my student-teacher suit. I'm short and slight. I look young, even for someone who's twenty-two. Wearing a suit and tie is the only way I can visibly exert any kind of presence in front of 8th and 9th grade English students.

Every morning, I try not to puke and not to touch the red stuff. Sometimes I fail.

In twenty years I'll have an alchemical cocktail that keeps the bolts turned tight—Divalproex for mania and migraines, even if it slurs my words and causes my fingers to vibrate steadily as I write on the board. Bupripon for depression. Amphetam to lift me back up from the Divalproex, which also causes depression. Careful dosages, specific times, a brittle biochemical balance.

But at twenty-two I have Visine and a headache and a roommate. He likes to smoke a joint when he's sitting on the toilet, thumbing biker porn, pages falling to the scuffed black-and-green linoleum and forming an R-rated, glossy bathmat. He hides the pot from me, although the veil of secrecy has never been Manhattan-Project thick. This room is big enough to squeeze a toilet and sink into, if the toilet is slightly angled. Ventilation comes through a window that opens only halfway and looks out on a trash-covered hillside. There's no fan. Just pot stink, floor porn, and a creeping red menace.

I stand in the shower and revolve slowly, keeping both sides under the warm spray. The bathroom's as cold as a beer cooler, and a layer of gray ice sometimes forms in the toilet overnight. The landlord loves "them Asian kids" because they pay the whole semester at once, and he won't fix the heat. Water pounds my head, painful on my scalp, as I think in slow, sluggish motion. My eyes throb, tiny bellows pumping pain into the space behind my forehead.

I don't feel like a million bucks this morning, any morning.

I feel like a cum covered $5 bill in a stripper's g-string, exhausted and sick and undiagnosed and a little drunk and dancing a sort of naked two-step as I make up my day's lesson plan entirely on the fly.

As the hot water runs low, something catches my eye, something just below the lever that controls the water's flow and temperature. It looks like a rust stain on the wall. I squint through the spray, realize that something's depending from the worn chrome.

I squat, lean in nearsightedly, let out a small beer fart.

It's some of the red stuff. Apparently, it has evolved.

Before, it was just growing on the shower pan, parts of the toilet, the piss- and porn-covered floor. Now it has become something that can dangle and sway gently in the mist—a long sheet of furry red shampoo gel hanging in the air.

The shock of being two inches from this evolved version of the red moss/mold/fungus hits me, and my stomach rolls. Slowly. Twice. My legs cramp. I retch, the muscles of my abdomen locked tight. With the third retch, I stand up, arms rigid out before me, palms flat on the wall.

As I stand and retch and think about pink bubblegum moss in my face and broken heaters and self-medication and biker porn, a burst of shit, powerful and over before I realize what's even happened, sprays the shower wall with an audible splat, like wet laundry dropped to a concrete floor. I glance down, look back over my shoulder, look away. Shit water swirls around my feet. Shit covers the wall behind me in a shotgun-scatter pattern.

I don't look again.

There's nothing else I can call this. This is shit. It isn't a turd. It isn't poop. It's not some hangover sloppy ploppy that got away from me. It's just shit, and Hallmark does not make a card for this moment.

It's a hopeless, helpless, desperate, lonely, angry, stupid shit smell. The smell of depression. I'm twenty-two years old and am judged highly by my supervising teacher. She adopts retired greyhounds and thinks I have good control over both my subject matter and my teenage students. She hasn't been around when I've lost my temper in class. She doesn't see me standing in the cold, naked, dry heaving, and not even in control of my own body.

I lean my head against the cool white wall, shiver, make do for twenty years.

In a wide ranging discussion of things that are scary (beginning with clowns and spiders, naturally), my daughter mentioned to me that she's sometimes afraid of the monsters under her bed.

I commiserated: "Sam, I totally understand. I'm pretty afraid of the monsters under your bed, too."

I was alright with turning 30, probably because I was so lousy at being twenty-anything. It just didn't seem traumatic, probably because nothing much changed except the demographic advertisers lumped me into. Turning 35 wiped me out. My career took an unexpected professional turn, as I moved from a teaching position focused only on undergraduates to one focused almost entirely on upper-division students and PhD candidates. I began trying to live better—less drinking, more active attention to the depression that's always deviled me. More attention to my wife and our new family. That's what slapped me around: defining my new role as a father, something I'd just never planned for.

2-9-2006: Inconclusive Conclusions

I DON'T KNOW what I expected to feel at this point in my life, largely because I never expected to reach this point at all. My first suicide attempt came in my early teens, and my drinking was daily before I finished high school; I wasn't making any real long term plans for the future. My lifestyle itself simply precluded such thoughts.

Yet here I am, 35 years old and the father of twins. I'm on the tenure track again, and I seem to be off to a solid start. I am, on the ranking system used in my department, Commendable. Not good enough for Excellent, not un-good enough for Satisfactory or Unsatisfactory. I can live with Commendable. Commendable feels like a ranking with a future. I only got her five months ago, after all.

It's been almost a year since *Trauma and the Teaching of Writing* was released, the reviews have been largely complimentary, and I've come to terms with the typographical error on the first page of its introduction. My writing textbook *The Promise of America* limps towards completion, and my collection of essays on the career perils of being an untenured administrator—a book that should be dedicated to

Gonzaga University and the faculty who inspired me—is on schedule. Both should go to the publisher in full manuscript form some time in the next few months.

I should be happy. Should at least *feel* happy.

That emotion isn't really on the table, though. Only when my wife and I spend quiet time together or when I play with my children do I feel anything that smacks of happiness.

Mostly, I feel like a failure—a feeling that comes with its twin bags of anger and shame.

I never expected to live this long and gave no thought to what being 35 and a father and married and successful would feel like.

I guess I'll live with it.

Rummaging through a toy box, my daughter gives me a play-by-play on what she's thinking, which seems to likely involve scaring her brother. Her plans often move in that orbit.

"Why," I asked, "are you talking baby talk?" (I have a thing about that.)

"Because I am wearing a Dracula cape."

I can't argue with that logic. I really can't.

*Part of me, a large part, is depressed by change. On some
level, I seem to accept Peter Straub's point from Ghost Story
that change is, by definition, always change for the worse.
That's ridiculous. But it explains why I'm so easily brought
down by the wind-caused death of a tree in my backyard.*

The Grass Will Grow

One taste of the old time sets all to rights.
—Robert Browning, "Childe Rolande to the Dark Tower Came"

AT NEARLY MIDNIGHT, as I'm drinking my third Budweiser and taping
Poison Ivy off HBO, both of my children suddenly begin to scream.
They're just a couple months shy of being two years old, so their lives
are all about extremes.

Every bump is an owie.

Every joy—from the taste of chocolate milk to the curly feel of our
poodle Ike's fur—is a wide, toothy grin. The extremes are all about
direct pain or joy.

They don't have any concept of abstract loss. Not yet.

Nixon, the cat I've had for nearly fourteen years, disappeared
just after New Years. I walked the neighborhood calling her name.
I knocked on doors and asked questions of neighbors I don't care to
know. I put up posters and called Animal Control.

But she's gone, and the kids don't know to miss her. Nixon's absence
is an extreme that they can't yet process.

So they scream, now, in total, absolute, abject terror over, quite
likely, nothing. I nearly break my shoulder on the doorframe, running into their room. Just today we baby-proofed the room in a big
way, big enough that they're now allowed unsupervised access to
their bedroom. So the geography of the place is strange again to me.

I trip on something that begins to sing "Old Dan Tucker" in an absurdly high-pitched voice that makes me think of spiders—the associative power of three beers and fear.

Sam's awake, rolling between her stuffed bears and howling. She's had a nightmare, I guess, although I don't know what toddlers have to terrorize their sleep.

Everything, I suppose.

Her screams have wakened her brother, who also begins to howl, his tiny face crunched into a fist-like rictus of toddler terror that hurts my heart. I cup Sam into my arms, where she cuddles into my chest. I hold my hand out to John, meaning to soothe him with a palm to the brow, and he shinnies up my arm like a monkey on a stick, also nestling against my chest.

I drop into the glider rocker we keep in their room for night-time reading comfort. They both relax immediately. Sam burrows her head into my armpit, socking her thumb squarely into her mouth. John wraps his already strong arms around my neck and rests his head on my shoulder.

Both of them fall asleep. The absolute trust they have in me seems so misplaced that it brings a large, fuzzy lump to my throat. I don't deserve this moment of total, absolute, guiltless, blameless, guileless, careless love and peace. I can't afford it.

I rock my twins, the taste of Budweiser in my mouth, and think of calling to my wife. The crying and my clumsiness didn't wake her up, but I could use some help standing and getting the kids back into their cribs.

I'm up and moving again, Sam screaming and waking John up. This time she's managed to shove her right leg through the bars of her crib so far that she can't pull it back out.

I shove her leg out, swaddle her in her pink blanket—a gift from the mother of one of the adjuncts at Gonzaga University—and she immediately falls back asleep. John's awake and upset, again, though. I tell him to lie down and, surprising us both I think, he does.

Standing beside his crib in the dark, listening to Sam's breathing, I stroke his head. It's warm to the touch, covered in slowly thickening hair that's so blonde it's almost white—like my hair, until a year or two after Stacie died.

I stroke his head in the dark, my cheek pressed against the edge of his crib's railing, crooning nonsense sounds to soothe him. It works.

Sitting on my back stoop, a bottle in my hand, I listen for my children's cries. The room they still share has its window right next to the patio, so I can hear every sound they make. I've taken two drinks from this bottle, making enough space to drop in a tiny piece of rock salt. I've never met anyone who salted their beer who wasn't also from Montana. This is my last beer of the night, and I may not even finish.

I'm just not very thirsty any more.

My parents are visiting for a week, mostly to see their grandchildren, of course. They'll be here some time late tomorrow, since we're more than ten hours away from Washington, even if the roads are good and there's no construction delay. Once he gets here, my father and I will pull down the only tree in my back yard—work that I hope we can manage without smashing my roof.

I'd pull the thing down myself—either the entire tree or the offending branch—if I wasn't concerned about my house or possibly cutting my fingers off with my chainsaw. A good friend from graduate school injured himself with a chainsaw less than a month ago, so such an accident is fresh in my mind.

Two nights back, as my twins slept and I wrote at my desk, a massive windstorm blew through. It tipped my garbage over, shook my fence alarmingly, and tore a large branch almost entirely away from the trunk of the tree in my back yard.

It would have been better for the tree if the branch had broken entirely away. Better for the tree but worse for me: If it had broken away clean, then the branch would likely have come through my office window. Instead, the weight of the limb—still 1/3 attached to the trunk—pulled all the way down, first stripping a long, deep line of bark and then digging a trench that touches all the way to the core.

The tree's dead and just hasn't realized it yet. It needs to come down.

I'm glad my father will be here to help. I need someone to keep me from getting hurt.

I'd planned to hang a tire swing from this tree once John and Sam were old enough not to fall from such a semi-dangerous, unstable thing. Now, instead, I'll fill in the round-shaped stump hole with dirt and nutrient-rich lawn soil that I buy by the bag.

I'll plant grass and tend it.

Within a couple years all traces of the fallen tree will be gone.

I teach writing. A lot of writing. I taught my first college-level writing class in 1993, and before that, I co-taught multiple writing and literature classes with an English professor, Dr. Donald Goodwin, who was my role model in the beginning. I warn my students on day one that I proceed through narrative digression…a nice way of saying I talk too much and tell too many stories. I even put the warning right on my syllabus now, just in the interest of full disclosure. I've been a teacher virtually all of my adult life, and I've been a father now for a decade (if we throw in the prep time encompassed by the IVF process). But before I was a father, and while I was just learning to be a professor, I became a husband. Somewhere in there, though, while I was teaching that first writing class, leaving a relationship behind, and heading (without knowing it) toward a fiancé, I struggled through the worst depression of my early adulthood.

"Want to meet my cat?"
partial draft, 2006

I don't know what his problems were, but he handled them by getting drunk every night.
— Larry McMurtry, *All My Friends Are Going to Be Strangers*

I SIT ON the sidewalk in front of my apartment and drink, my ass cold and brick digging into my back. Sometimes I sit here in the sun and read books about World War I, a new hobby I picked up the summer before starting graduate school. Mostly I just sit here at night and drift, a brown bottle close to hand.

My apartment only has two small rooms—plus a bathroom—so I can hear everything, even from outside. Ringing phone, a zombie movie on the television, Hamburger Helper sizzling on the stove. The smell of cooking hamburger goes badly with the smells of spiced rum and desperation. I rented this apartment, partially, to get away from the pot/porn/red fungus bathroom apartment I shared with a friend. It was a mistake. I don't miss the red fungus, but I can't really afford this tiny, over-priced place that I rent from an openly racist slum lord

I sit in the dark and drink and wait, listening to a movie play on the VCR and occasionally stirring the Cheeseburger Macaroni flavor that I always favor. Some nights, I simply cook an entire pound of bacon and eat that for dinner. No eggs. No potatoes. It's quiet in Cheney at night, when the only pleasant company is my buzz and the barking dog across the street. I hold the beer in my left hand, and I wait for the peace around me to encourage a peace within me.

I wait for the "click" that Tennessee Williams knew all about, the moment when alcohol finally turns off my lights.

I do this nearly every night for six months, drinking and mulling over bad choices. All choices. The only escape I have from this routine is teaching during the day and crashing at a friend's place on the weekend, until he graduates and goes off to find a teaching position.

It's not much of a life, and eventually I move to a cheaper apartment several blocks away—around a right-angle corner and completely out from under that first lonely apartment's sphere of influence. I move into a second-floor apartment in an old boarding house, one with a front porch big enough for several lawn chairs and an ash barrel. Classy.

A few months after moving there, I meet my wife.

Rob invites me to his party so that I won't call the police when the noise gets out of hand—he even brings a couple beers with him when we have our "I'm having a party tonight and I'd like you to come" conversation.

I drink his beer. I'm polite. I say I'll try to come to his party.

I have every intention of staying home, playing a new World War II strategy game I've purchased, drinking the case of Budweiser bottles that's cooling in my refrigerator. To hell with Rob and his party. He throws terrible parties. Just terrible. The last time I went, I walked into six people huddled around a kitchen table, not talking, drinking shots like they were personally angry at Jim Beam.

It was creepy.

I'm not dating anyone now and haven't been for months.

There's no Breanna tonight. No Carrie, Tricia, Mandy, Tayra, Cherie, Keri, Carrie II, Sara, Susan, Leyna, Devin, Desiree, Margot. No history professor's daughter or tall blonde from the Spokane Singles Line. No bank teller in her early thirties. No Air Force wife leaving her husband after fifteen years. No pothead roommate of the bartender at Goofy's Tavern. No MFA student who sleeps around and writes bad poetry about the bartender she loves who only loves her breasts, no undergraduates I met when I was their English teacher and then bumped into when they were drinking illegally in a bar, especially Showies.

There's just beer and Rob's invitation.

I thank Rob for inviting me to the party. We've been drunks together for years. We lived in the same dorm for a while, and he attended an introduction to fiction class that I co-taught. He's a good guy. I'm not going to his party.

I watch movies all night, watch until I'm drunk and bored and sweating in the summer heat. I have an air conditioning unit stuck into the window of my living room, but running it 24 hours per day still barely keeps the place livable. Part of the reason I sleep on the bathroom floor is that it's the coolest room in the house. That, and I tend to pass out there.

I drink beer, play with my cat Nixon, clean my apartment. The strategy game is cool but too complicated, too slow. I love computer games but was dumb enough to buy a Mac. It's a terrible computer for gaming.

Finally, just after ten o'clock, I put on a clean pair of jeans and a mostly clean shirt. I grab two beers out of my refrigerator, walk outside, sit in one of the partially sprung lawn chairs and finish one beer. I set it in a line of more than a dozen empty bottles, all of them mine, many from tonight. I open the second beer and knock on Rob's door.

The room's packed. I don't recognize anybody. I ask around for Rob, but no one knows where he is—or who he is, in some cases.

A group of girls, all under age, dance in the middle of the living room—some bumping and grinding sort of dance that seems to happen to the specific rhythm of the rap song that's playing. It's sexy in an innocent orgy sort of way. I hate rap and anyone who dances to it. My generation came of age on classic rock and the rise (and fall, more or less) of hair metal. Rap meant Vanilla Ice and "Parents Just Don't Understand"; rap never had a chance with those sorts of credentials.

I think about leaving and instead go out onto the patio to find Rob. I want him to know I showed up at his party tonight because I'll likely never come to another one.

He isn't there.

She is.

Elizabeth sits on a lawn chair at the edge of the patio, talking to friends from class. She's short, with hair to the middle of her back, and I'm so taken with her that I actually drop my beer when I see her. It doesn't break, but it lands with a glass-on-cement *clink*.

No one sees this happen, though, or hears it, and I walk away from the spinning, foaming bottle as quickly as possible.

Let Rob deal with it when he comes home, I figure.

I'm so drunk I can barely stand. I hunker next to Beth's chair, join the conversation. I single her out for attention, pull her away from the crowd, especially the bump and grind girls listening to the stereo. I'm drunk, and the details escape me as soon as they happen. At some point we begin talking about pets.

"Do you," I ask, "want to meet my cat?"

It may be the worst pickup line in the world. Maybe the worst in the *history* of the world.

It works. Maybe the power's in the delivery.

We go upstairs to my apartment. We meet my cat. I walk Elizabeth to her car some hours later and give her a hug goodbye.

The next day I receive a letter accepting for publication an article I've co-authored about teaching writing using scenes from popular movies. A phone call late in the afternoon tells me that I've been awarded a teaching assistantship that'll pay for the rest of my schooling, something I didn't think would happen.

Elizabeth and I have dinner at Willow Springs to celebrate.

Four months later we're engaged.

Just over a year later we're married.

I'm paranoid about safety (not my own—I'll take wicked risks with my own health—but not with my family's safety, which matters). Worried that our Fernley, Nevada, home was in a bad neighborhood, I paid ADT $1000 for a system I could have constructed myself with $100 at Target. And I worried about fire. Kids often hide when a fire breaks out, and I was terrified that such a thing might be done by John and Samantha. So we practiced fire safety.

Fire Drill
a largely complete draft that just never found a home

I HOLD JOHN's hand as we walk down the hall discussing fire. He's five. I'm trying to impress upon him how dangerous it can be if our house catches on fire and he needs to escape in the middle of the night. I warn him never, ever to hide under his bed or in his closet. I calmly but repeatedly tell him how important it is that he's responsible for himself and only for himself.

"John takes care of John," I say again and again as he asks me "what about" questions. What about his twin, Sam? What about mom and dad?

These seem like reasonable concerns, given his age. I don't even worry when he asks about the potential fiery fate of Ike and Frank— our dog and cat, respectively.

We sit on the living room floor and talk about fire, about stop-drop-and-roll techniques. I feel like Father of the Year. John's kindergarten teacher said it was homework to talk about fire safety. We have discussed fire safety. I rock fatherhood.

Then the questions continue: "What about Sara Bear? Can I take Sara Bear?" I nod, say "sure," try to move on with my description of the escape plan. But John's not done worrying about his plush green dinosaur with the incongruous name. "Can I go back for Sara? What if I can't find Sara."

John's seriously worried about Sara Bear, and my lesson has been shot to Hell.

"You let me worry about Sara, ok?"

His brown eyes focus on me, scan my face for a lie, somehow miss the fact that, in the event of a fire, Sara Bear is not on my priority list.

I give Samantha the same spiel, and she's much more up front with her major concern. When I tell her that "Sam takes care of Sam," she hugs Daddy Bear tight to her chest. I don't argue. There's no doubt in my mind that, in the event of a fire, she'll stop to get Daddy Bear before leaving the house.

We move on to the actual escape. I send them to their room after telling them what to do. Then I stand on a chair, push against the glowing green button, and yell: "Fire! Fire!"

They sprint from their rooms, dogleg down the laundry room hallway, and plough through into the garage. For a fire drill, there's an inordinate amount of giggling. John slams his little palm against the garage door opener, and they both scamper underneath the door as it rises. As planned, they run into the driveway, turn, and halt on the sidewalk.

Giggling and stuffed-animal concerns aside, these are two five year olds who are now more safe from fire than they were half an hour ago. This is a good thing, and I tell the kids how proud of them I am. It isn't easy to praise them, though.

I'm trying not to burst into tears, and I don't know why. My throat is so tight and thick with unshed tears that I can't breathe.

I mask my trouble by talking louder and more demonstrably—"Good job, guys! You did awesome! What a good job!"

My tone fluctuates wildly. I suspect that I sound like an asshole. I certainly feel like one.

I've digressed. Back to fatherhood. My daughter Samantha and I are alike in many ways, including our tendency to take things to extremes. These points of similarity started appearing pretty early on...

Stories in the Bank
journal entry ca. 2010

SAM AND I kneel across from one another, her piggy bank on the floor between us. It doesn't look like a pig, except in its vaguely bulbous, purse-like shape and odd pink color—a color so strange it can only exist in the bedroom of a five-year-old girl. If I touch it, it'll stain my fingers.

As I think this, Sam actually does reach out and touch the bank. Our minds often work in similar tracks, even though I'm forty. She gives it a shake, rattling the single bit of change left inside. We've dumped all of the rest out of the hole at the bottom of this pig-like bank—a ratcheting enema of copper and silver—leaving only one dollar, a silver time traveler from 1879 that I gave her in place of the Susan B. Anthony dollar her brother John wanted.

Right now, Sam and I want to get that dollar. It's too big to come out of the pig-purse's asshole. This leaves us with a problem that I should be able to solve.

"We could smash it," Sam says. She's right. We could. I'd like to do this, in fact, but, as the adult here, it seems like I should come up with a better plan than swinging a hammer.

I pick the bank up again and give it a couple more futile shakes, the dollar bouncing and jouncing and coming no closer to falling out. I look at the circle at the bottom and the slit at the top. Why is one able to accept a coin that won't come out the other? This seems like a serious engineering flaw.

If Sam was a guy my age, I'd shrug and say, "Sam, this is stupid."

I can't say that to a 5-year-old. Instead, I shake her pink pig purse bank a few more times, and, unsurprisingly, the dollar still doesn't fall out.

"You sure you don't want the hammer?"

I smile to myself. Questions like this confirm that Sam is my daughter.

I give the bank another futile shake. Suddenly a slip of paper drops out—white and rectangular with red words on one side. I glance at this fallout from a fortune cookie: Apparently, my Sam is the "master of every situation."

This is information I should know about my daughter, and it's an excellent distraction. She grabs the fortune and runs off to show it to her mother, leaving me on my knees with the almost-empty pig.

I stare at it, wishing for my hammer.

This is how I find the stories that matter: I shake one and another drops out.

I don't spend much time in bars anymore, which isn't really a shame. While I can drink like I did half a lifetime ago, I can't recover with the same speed. A couple beers while mowing the lawn shoots my night's REM sleep to hell. I tend to meet fewer mental incompetents, though, now that I'm not regularly polishing bartops with my elbows.

Schizos
an unfinished essay in two fragments

[O]utcasts who deal in extremes are bound to cause trouble.
—Hunter S. Thompson, *Hell's Angels*

I drink so I / can talk to assholes. / This includes me.
—James Douglas Morrison, "Road Days"

THE MINUTE I see him, back to the three of us, hunched over the bar at four o'clock in the afternoon, red coat torn and smeared with dirt, I know he's trouble. Even sitting on a stool and facing away from me, it's obvious that he's nearly too drunk to stand.

The room's empty, except for him and us. Even the bartender isn't around, which is bad. When a bartender doesn't hang out to talk with the only customer in the place, things aren't right.

No one else seems to notice the guy, and I don't say anything. Although I see trouble, I also don't see any reason to raise the alarm. Jack wanders toward a table on the far side of the room, Jamie following. There's something British about Jack, something I can't put my finger on. But it gives him an air of authority, so I defer to his table choice, just like I defer to his wisdom and experience whenever he makes a comment in one of the classes we share. Jamie wears a battered leather jacket and seems tough, even if she does study the Romantic poets. She isn't. When the drama starts, she'll run for the bathroom.

I don't know this, though, and sit with my back almost to the bar—just turned sideways enough that I can see Red Coat. As I sit down, Jamie calls for the waitress. Red Coat notices us, and I see him debating his options. If he chooses anything other than staying on his stool, I'll be unhappy.

The waitress brings our drinks and disappears. Before I even get the bottle to my lips for the first time, Red Coat's standing across from me.

"Can I sit with you?" He's talking to all of us but looking at me. So I feel bound to answer for all of us.

"Nah," I say in the friendliest tone I can manage. "We work together and wanna talk shop. Thanks, though." *Hell am I thanking him for?*

He doesn't move. Just stares at me. I feel a drop of sweat roll down my side and suppress a shudder. Dimly realizing we're not welcoming him to our group, he sweetens his proposed deal: "Ok if I sit? I used to work for the government and know a lot of classified shit." He actually manages to puff up a bit as he says this.

Part of me is tempted. I'm curious to know what sort of classified shit he thinks he knows—or what kind of lies he's willing to spin for me. I like lies. Good ones.

Jack jumps in before I can let my curiosity win out.

"We work together," Jack says, echoing my assertion, "and we just want to relax. Long day, you know?" Even this sounds British to me, authoritative.

"I'll get ya a round," Red Coat slurs, ignoring our dismissal, our disinterest in his insider knowledge of classified shit. He walks off, angling across the empty dance floor, looking for the waitress. Jamie stands up without saying a word and walks toward the bathroom. Jack just sits. Neither reaction is helpful, so I follow Red Coat into the restaurant portion of the place, where he's cornered a waitress and is telling her to bring us drinks, on his tab.

She's looking through him, not even nodding.

When he turns to go back into the bar, he nearly runs into me. I step around him as he stumbles off, and I cancel the order. "We don't want his drinks," I say.

The waitress is blonde and maybe eighteen years old, probably the daughter of the bar's owner. She's seen me here before and knows I'm not much trouble, although I have a tendency to get pissy if it takes an inordinate amount of time for my drink to come. When I talk to her, I'm close enough to smell the Dove soap on her skin: "Call the police. There's about to be a fight."

I don't know why I add this last sentence, and I don't know if Red Coat hears me. I don't know that it's almost the exact same wording I'll use two decades later, almost fighting over a parking space. When I get back to our table, Jamie is still gone, and Jack looks like a fish caught in a lantern beam. He's just sitting, watching Red Coat pack his things. From nowhere, this guy's produced a brown briefcase, and he's got it open. Thankfully, he's putting things into it rather than taking them out—so I'm guessing he doesn't have a knife or gun, a possibility that never occurred to me until now.

"You know what happens to guys like you in prison?" he asks me. I sigh. I know this dance. He's taken the first step. I have to take the second. It never occurs to me not to.

"Get out of here," I say. That's actually pretty diplomatic, I think, in retrospect. I'm standing next to my chair, the table partially between us.

Remarkably, he picks up his case and begins to leave.

I don't sigh with relief, but I sink into my chair and begin to take a drink from the brown, slowly warming bottle. The bottle that still hasn't made it to my lips once.

Before he reaches the door, Red Coat sets his briefcase on the floor, turns around, and charges me. As he charges, he lets out the loudest, strangest battle cry I can even imagine—a sort of "yeah" sound, pulled long in the middle and punctuated by his pounding feet.

He's flying at me from the far side of the room, just flailing arms and stomping feet. With each wild step, his knees seem to come almost up to his nipples.

I very nearly shit myself before adrenaline and subconscious survival instincts kick in.

I stand so fast that my chair tips over, hitting the back of my knees, and I grab my beer by its neck, reversing it and drawing it back to swing. I figure I can get two or three good hits in before we reach the floor—bottles only break in movies. In the non-cinematic world, a bottle is a good bludgeon, the kind of thing that builds stories ending with trips to the ER and stitches. Hit a guy with a bottle for real and it nearly tears his head off. Beer running down my arm and foaming in a cool puddle on the floor, I stand and wait.

Red Coat just fucked with the wrong English professor.

He stops running and screaming at the exact same moment, like someone kicked his plug out of the wall. Doesn't say a word. Turns, grabs his briefcase. Leaves.

I look at Jack, who is also standing. He shrugs.

The waitress doesn't see any of this. Jamie doesn't come back to the table for another ten minutes. When the cops come by, nearly two hours later, they don't even question me or Jack. I hear them tell the owner that they put the guy, a well-known schizophrenic, apparently, on a bus out of town.

They all nod at each other like this is a solution.

I sit, drink, and wonder if the poor Greyhound rider next to him is now getting to hear all the confidential shit I missed out on.

The bartender's doing her routine, setting up for the night's trade. At three o'clock in the afternoon, however, there's no hurry. The bar's deserted, other than the two of us and a piano in the corner that's playing with itself. That might be cool if the keys were at least going up and down, but they are motionless. So, effectively, the piano has become nothing but a 400 lbs. speaker.

I've got a book open in front of me, stretched open with my left hand. I'm at a conference in Kentucky, presenting at a semi-annual gathering of scholars in rhetoric and composition. My graduate students are out seeing the town. I never bother sightseeing when I'm traveling for work. Find my room, the conference site, and a bar. Then I'm good.

My right hand never strays far from the cool bottle of beer sitting before me, a napkin wrapped around it and held in place by condensation.

I'm not looking at the book. Not much. Mostly I'm watching the bartender as she bends over to check inside cabinets and coolers, stretches on her tip-toes to reach things on high shelves.

Her red hair hangs past her waist in a tight ponytail, and her southern accent is so pronounced I question its authenticity.

She reminds me too much of Blanche Dubois to be real. In the space of maybe twenty minutes she's referred to me as *honey, sweety, darlin'*, and *baby*.

Baby.

I wouldn't tolerate this sort of name calling from anyone but a redheaded bartender.

I hear the door open, but the bartender doesn't take her eyes off her work and I don't take my eyes off her. I only look when the smell reaches me.

He's my size, maybe ten years older. Grayed hair, dirty and greasy and long. He hoists himself onto the bar's corner stool with a grunt and a mutter that I can't quite understand. His stink—onions and sweat and the streets—gets to me before the bartender notices him.

She makes no move to serve him, ignores him by turning her attention fully to polishing glasses and opening and closing cupboards behind the bar. I turn my attention to my book, trying not to stare at her or to smell him.

He waits, muttering in a soft voice that's almost inaudible beneath the sounds of running water and piano music. I keep watch from the corner of my eye.

A sense of menace, of impending violence or argument surrounds this guy.

"Hey." I glance at him, confirming that he's not talking to me. He's not. Instead, he's summoning the bartender—tiny and redheaded and alone except for me. We'd been discussing Bill Murray movies before this guy and his stink arrived, her cleaning and me drinking my way through her last three bottles of Nut Brown Ale, brewed right across the street from the bar.

She turns to him and tilts her head to the left, acknowledging his call but taking no steps toward him.

I feel protective of her.

He's got her attention, but he repeats himself before moving on: "Hey. Hey. How much for a brewskie?"

"What?" I'm not sure if she understands him or just can't hear him. He repeats himself, repeats his question in its entirety.

"Hey. Hey. How much for a brewskie?"

"A beer?"

"Yeah. Hey."

Hey seems to be some sort of verbal hangup for this guy, almost as annoying as the smell.

She checks the price. "Six dollars." She goes back to opening and closing cupboards on the far side of the bar.

"Hey. How much for a drink?"

"Nine dollars." She doesn't even look at him.

"Hey. How much for a glass of wine?"

"Twelve dollars." He mutters especially loudly about this. I'm sure he says *fucking shit*. Pretty sure, any way.

"Gimme water. Hey. With lemon. No. With lime."

I'm barely even pretending to read by now, fully engrossed in the dance between my bartender and Price Check. I'm worried about her. It's just the two of us here, and poor hygiene isn't this guy's only problem. The last thing I want is for him to sit near me with a glass in his hand.

My bartender scoops ice into a glass. I notice that she uses an actual metal scoop to fill the glass rather than shoving the glass itself into the ice. That's dangerous; I was taught never to scoop that way, as was, apparently, she.

Glasses break when they're used as scoops. People can get cut.

The bartender hands him his ice, drops a twist of lime in it. As she walks to the far side of the bar, we make eye contact.

Blanche looks scared. I probably do, too. I don't know if she's been in this situation before or not, but I have.

I take a long drink from my beer, keeping the bottle close at hand. I don't have anything else to hit with.

Another freakin' schizo, I think. *What're the odds?*

Of course, writing that rhetorical question—"What're the odds?"—I had no idea that I had a lifetime of psycho-meeting ahead of me. Psychotics at the bus stop babbling about a bicycle with no guard over the tire to keep "road muckness" from shooting up onto the driver, talking non-stop while I wait for the Number 7 to rescue me. A panhandler in Atlanta who bet me $5 that he could tell me where I "got" my shoes; before I could say a word, he cackled, "You got them on your feet!" He demanded the $5 I hadn't wagered and only gave up when I casually slid my black leather jacket open and moved my right hand slowly around to the small of my back. "Don't shoot me," he said as he backed away...and I gripped nothing but my belt. At least it keeps things interesting, I guess, being a weirdness magnet.

Because Mistakes Were Made *begins with some of my previously published work, it seems only appropriate to end with something that started on the road to publication, took a couple steps, then fizzled out when I began to wonder (a) if I was saying anything parents needed to hear and (b) if I had a point at all. That same thing happens to me a lot in the classroom, where I warn my students, on day one, that I have a tendency to talk too much. I call this approach to education my Pedagogy of Narrative Digression...*

Conclusion: On Soccer and Unpublished Drafts
October 2014

Anything can be an instrument, Chigurh said. Small things. Things you wouldn't even notice. They pass from hand to hand. People don't pay attention. And then one day there's an accounting. And after that nothing is the same.

—Cormac McCarthy, *No Country for Old Men*

I'VE BEEN THROWN out of more than a few places over the years:
    A Spokane, Washington, strip club, for example, where a friend was celebrating his bachelor party. Technically, I wasn't really thrown out. When I learned that the place didn't sell alcohol—only soda at $7 per glass—I walked next door to a bar that did, conveniently enough, sell alcohol. I walked back and forth several times. Then the bouncer at the club put his hand on my chest—a hand big enough to cover much of my chest—and told me to go away. I make it a policy not to argue with men taller, heavier, and younger (and sober when I am not). The bouncer at the bar had no problem with my coming back

in. His name was Jeff. He was majoring in mechanical engineering. We were the only two in the bar, and we talked for an hour while my friend ended his bachelorhood.

A nineteen-year-old Korean once threw me out of his apartment after inviting me to a party he was throwing, but, in his defense, I was too drunk by the time I even arrived to do more than lean against the refrigerator and grope his girlfriend. He presented a pretty reasonable position (as he took his lady friend by the hand and pulled her away from me): "You go now! Now!" Spit actually flew from his lips, he yelled this with such force, and hit me on the cheek. I came to in the morning on my living room floor, just far enough into the room to have kicked the door closed behind me before I fell. So obviously I went "now"—I just didn't last long. Considering that I was his guest, it's lucky he didn't send me back to my apartment by bum rushing me over the balcony rail. The parking lot would have broken my fall.

A schizophrenic Vietnam Vet threw me out of his tent on Superbowl Sunday, back in maybe 1991. He was a Buffalo fan. I wasn't. We had denominational differences that alcohol didn't smooth over.

Three sorority sisters threw me out of their Halloween party once, probably because my apartment was less than twenty feet from their house, and at my place, the loud noise never stopped. When I staggered through their front door, they were huddled together in a group, dancing in place to Madonna and drinking strawberry wine straight from the bottle they were passing. One of them, the only one who wasn't blonde, pointed at me, and two large fraternity boys frog-marched me back onto the porch as I sputtered out sentence fragments beginning with "What?" and "Hey!" They weren't as big as the strip club bouncer, but there were two of them. To balance the scales of justice, I soccer-kicked all of the carefully carved pumpkins that decorated the porch out into the parking lot. No one did anything to stop me, probably because it was such a freakish yet audacious act of pointless aggression. The pumpkin shrapnel lay in an arc around the porch for months, gently rotting and bringing a smile to my lips as I walked to and from class.

I found myself thinking about this last incident of forced ejection from a social gathering today. Not the parking lot. Not the pumpkins. The soccer kick. And the pointless aggression.

My kids play local soccer. My wife—a much better person than I, a person who has never been thrown out of anyplace—coaches their team, just as she did last year. She's pretty good at it, leading the kids through age-appropriate drills and rotating everyone in and out of games in a logical and fair way. The one time I had to fill in for her, I realized I didn't even know anyone's name. I just pointed and yelled useful things like "Get in there!" and "Good effort!"

That last one's especially useful, since it applies to a situation where something good or bad has happened equally well.

During today's game at the field by the local YMCA, though, I wandered away to get something to drink. I'm no coffee snob, so something that's been sitting in a pot simmering itself into oblivion in the Y's lounge area is fine with me. Returning to the sidelines, I stood midfield, clutching my Styrofoam cup and wondering what the score might be.

I tend to ignore the folks around me—not out of rudeness but simply because when I attend a sporting event, I'm actually there to watch the sporting event and not to gossip with people I see regularly in other venues. Especially if I'm watching my kids. They like having me around, but they like to know I'm paying attention to what they're doing, too.

That's as far as the draft went.

Not even that far, really. The original draft cut off after "The soccer kick." But the other paragraphs at the end were scribbled down in a notebook I carry, the latest in a series of small notebooks that I've packed around with me for fifteen years. I can see easily enough where I was going with all of this: When I came back from the YMCA, coffee in my hand, I ended up standing close to the opposing team.

As I stood there watching the game, I realized that the coach was complaining, bitterly and incessantly, about my wife's team. Specifically, she was complaining that the kids kept all rushing into the goal-tender's box. I guess there's a rule against this, but I know even less about soccer than I know about thermodynamics, ancient Sumerian religious practices, or the geography of the Land of Nod (which I at least think might be to the west of Eden…).

I have no problem with complaining about sporting events, especially when the complaints are about broken rules that aren't being enforced. But I also have a general guideline that I expect everyone to follow: If you're sitting on my couch and complaining about the referees at an NFL game, then I'm perfectly happy to listen to you complain. If you're standing on the sidelines at a children's sporting event being refereed by volunteers, either say something to the refs or shut up.

So the coach kept complaining, and I kept drinking my coffee, waiting to see if she was going to say something to the local teens who were refereeing the match. She wasn't. Instead, she was inciting the parents of her team's players, getting them all fired up about the injustice of a broken rule (in a game that they were winning, any way). One of the fathers sidled closer to me and repeated what the coach was spouting: My wife's team wasn't staying out of the goalie's box. They were breaking the rules. The ref wasn't calling it.

I snapped. A little. "Yeah," I agreed. "They're breaking *a* rule, not rules. They're also eight years old, and it's the second game of the season."

This was pretty diplomatic for me, really. I didn't swear, even. He scuttled away without a word, and I didn't watch him go. He must have gone to the coach, though, to complain about me…because suddenly she was standing by my side, closer than social norms really call for, restating her points.

I was going to ignore her. But she made it personal, ending with "Your wife's coached for four years. She should know better."

I snapped. A lot.

"That's amazing," I said louder than I needed to, "since we haven't even lived in Montana for four years, and she didn't coach at all the first year we were here." She tried to respond, and I just got a little louder. I'm a teacher. I can project my voice when called to do so. "If you've got a problem with the rules, then talk to the refs. Don't just stand here and bitch and moan about it."

More accurately, I probably said, "If you've got a problem with the rules, then talk to the refs! Don't just stand here and bitch and moan about it!"

"You can go stand over there," she responded, making shooing gestures with her hands.

"I'm fine here."

And being the prick I am, I stood there for the rest of the game.

That was the whole story, not counting the vague fallout: I still see that coach all of the time. Her kids are the same age as my twins. I see her with her own kid when I'm dropping mine off at birthday parties and picking them up from swim team. I see her at flag football. I'll see her again at soccer, even if my wife chooses not to coach this coming season (since the kids will still choose to play, I'm sure).

Every time I see her, I smile and say hello (again, because I'm something of a prick but also because I don't hold a grudge over nonsense). She doesn't respond. She gives me an "I hate you" look. She can hate me if she wants to do so. It seems like a waste of emotional energy to me. Plus, I've been hated by professionals, so a Montana soccer mom doesn't much rattle my cage.

The whole point I'd have argued in this piece was, I guess, about sports, about parents being too fired up by what their kids are doing. I get too fired up sometimes, though, and I've written about the topic before.

Worse, the draft was of an article for a parenting magazine...and it opens with an extended description of places I've been thrown out of, all of them while I was drunk. It could, as approaches go, fit the audience, if the parents reading the piece were as badly behaved in their youth as I was. But it wouldn't fit the genre especially well, since it's too much about me and not enough about kids or parenting or anything. It's just about a dad behaving badly…before he was ever a dad. Long before.

The stories at the beginning connect to the soccer-game anecdote only loosely, only because that coach tried to throw me out of the game. That's the association that sent my mind down this particular narrative track.

I like those stories, even though I don't come off especially well in them.

I like the soccer anecdote, even though it repeats a vague lesson that's been taught before.

Publishing it would have been a mistake.

Maybe.

Favorite moments/quotations from today's football game (which John and Sam's team won by a touchdown):

Sam's coach gives specific instructions to Player A, specific instructions to Player B, and then tells Sam…"Just get in there and wreak havoc."

Another time: "John, swing around the left. Sam, go straight up the middle." That one led to a sack.

Most frequently overheard line from the opposing coach: "You! [Point to any of his players, sometimes more than one.] Cover that girl!"

The Backlist of Previously Published Work

in order of appearance, more or less

"Shoot the Drift" first appeared in the online journal *Brevity: A Journal of Concise Literary Nonfiction.*

"Sleep Deprivation, Drunkenness, and Dr. Phil" first appeared in *Montana Parent* magazine.

"Dad's Here?" first appeared in *TWINS.*

"On Twins and Kitchen Safety" first appeared in *TWINS.*

"Peter Benchley is Dead" first appeared in *Fourth Genre.*

"Icky Papa Died" first appeared in the online journal *Brevity: A Journal of Concise Literary Nonfiction.*

"On Being Thankful" first appeared in the online publication *MyTwinLink*.com.

"Not Far From Montana" first appeared in *Fernley News*, and a similar story/argument appears in the introduction to *The Cost of Business.*

"Of Nails, Nonfiction, and Various Adhesives" first appeared in the Craft section of *Brevity: A Journal of Concise Literary Nonfiction.*

"Push" first appeared in *Whitefish Review.*

"Similar Differences" first appeared in *Montana Parent* magazine.

"Becoming that Dad" first appeared in *Montana Parent* magazine.

"Games, Movies, and Childhood Magic" first appeared in *Montana Parent* magazine.

"At the Corner of Cornell and Crazy" first appeared in *Gum in Your Hair: A Blog for Parents Under the Big Sky.*

"Private? Or Secret?" first appeared in *Montana Parent* magazine.

"My Son's First Pair of Cowboy Boots" first appeared in *Gum in Your Hair: A Blog for Parents Under the Big Sky.*

"My Wrapping Privileges May Be Revoked" first appeared in *Gum in Your Hair: A Blog for Parents Under the Big Sky.*

"Documentary Evidence" first appeared in *Gum in Your Hair: A Blog for Parents Under the Big Sky.*

"Memories, Nightmares, and Sin" first appeared in *Gum in Your Hair: A Blog for Parents Under the Big Sky.*

"Save, Saving, Saved" first appeared in *Gum in Your Hair: A Blog for Parents Under the Big Sky.*

"On Time" first appeared in *Gum in Your Hair: A Blog for Parents Under the Big Sky.*

"You Promised" first appeared in *Gum in Your Hair: A Blog for Parents Under the Big Sky.*

"New Normal" first appeared in *Gum in Your Hair: A Blog for Parents Under the Big Sky.*

"Education for Irrelevance" first appeared in *Gum in Your Hair: A Blog for Parents Under the Big Sky.*

About the Author

Shane Borrowman teaches writing and editing...plus popular literature and studies in horror cinema, particularly zombie films from 1935 to 2010. He earned a BAE and two MAs from Eastern Washington University and a PhD from The University of Arizona. Since 2001, he has taught at Gonzaga University, the University of Nevada, Reno, and the University of Montana Western, where he serves as English Department Chair.

Shane left Montana several days after graduating from high school and didn't come back for 23 years. He drove out of Montana with his best friend, his love of macro-beer, and his 1981 Chevy Citation. Returning, he brought with him a profession, a family, and an inexplicable hatred for one specific (former) New England Patriots' quarterback.

As Dr. Borrowman, he is editor or co-editor of multiple books, including *Trauma and the Teaching of Writing*, *On the Blunt Edge*, and *The Cost of Business*—and author or co-author of dozens, possibly even scores, of articles (on topics ranging from teaching writing to the history of boxing to medieval studies of Arabic Aristotelians). He is probably the only living writer to publish in *Fourth Genre* and to win *Rhetoric Review*'s "best article of the year" award, The Rupert Radford Trust Award. (Those two things did not happen in the same year. Or even in the same decade, actually. That would have been even more cool.)

His office is less than 70 miles from the Butte, Montana, hospital where he was born. This gives him great pleasure. As the last member of his family in this piece of the world, the responsibility for a significant amount of grave maintenance has dropped into his lap; awash in memories of a Montana childhood where he was surrounded by his great grandmother, most of her eleven children, and their own extended families—plus his father's people—this lived experience has led into a lot of memoir. The current manuscript of stories about these people, long loved and long gone, begins, "When I visit the dead, I take a lawn chair."

Mistakes Were Made was built for his mother, originally, as a Mother's Day present...but every essay was written for his twins, Samantha and John. Even the ones that will embarrass them.

Made in the USA
Las Vegas, NV
14 March 2022

45665230R00121